The Ills of Aid

The Ills of Aid

An Analysis of Third World
Development Policies

Eberhard Reusse

The University of Chicago Press
Chicago and London

#48966728

EBERHARD REUSSE worked for three decades for the United Nations Food and Agriculture Organization and other international and bilateral development programs, including numerous World Bank investment missions.

The University of Chicago Press, Chicago 60637
The University of Chicago Press, Ltd., London

© 1999, 2002 by Institut für Entwicklungsforschung und Entwicklungspolitik, Bochum

Foreword by Vernon W. Ruttan © 2002 by The University of Chicago
Foreword by Paul Streeten © 2002 by The University of Chicago

11 10 09 08 07 06 05 04 03 02   1 2 3 4 5
ISBN: 0-226-71014-9 (cloth)

CIP data is available.

To FAO and all my former colleagues, especially my mentor
John Abbott, for opening the world to me

Contents

Foreword

Eberhard Reusse has written a provocative book. He draws on extensive experience and scholarship in the field of development assistance to challenge the conventional wisdom that has guided assistance to the world's poorest countries, particularly in Africa, during the 1980s and 1990s.

Reusse's critique focuses on two closely related assistance programs—the war on waste and cereal banks. The war on waste was motivated by a perception of very substantial postharvest losses—in storage, transportation, and distribution—both at the village level and in marketing channels. The cereal banks program was motivated by a perception that food security could be enhanced and exploitation by traders could be reduced by the establishment of collectively managed village-level food-storage programs. Neither program was based on careful consultation with villagers about their needs or on adequate professional assessments of program costs and benefits. Large resources were devoted to the programs. Implementation, often by nongovernmental organizations, was poorly managed. Program monitoring and evaluation by donors were inadequate. After almost two decades of effort donors have finally become disillusioned with the results and are withdrawing support. The observations by Reusse are largely consistent with my own earlier observations regarding agricultural credit and rural development programs in Asia.

What conclusions should be drawn from the evidence presented by Reusse? Some critics have argued that development assistance, as it has been conceived and managed since the 1950s, is no longer viable. Some view this as a cause for celebration. But I do not share this conclusion. And I view with concern the evidence of "aid weariness" and the declining assistance budgets of the developed-country donors and of international assistance agencies. There are a number of reforms, some of them outlined by Reusse, that would contribute to more productive assistance programs.[1]

I doubt, however, that the reforms that are needed, both at the project level discussed by Reusse and at the macro- and sector levels, will occur. In retrospect it is clear that much of the economic-assistance effort, until well into the 1990s, was driven by Cold War tensions. The Cold War order has been replaced by a new world disorder. I am skeptical that calls will be made for a new and more effective development-assistance effort until the leaders of the developed world are able to capture and articulate a clearer vision of a kinder and more prosperous world order. The great danger is that the developed countries will decide to retreat into a "fortress world" in which relations with

---

1. I have also advanced a series of reform suggestions in *U.S. Development Assistance Policy: The Domestic Politics of Foreign Economic Aid* (Baltimore: Johns Hopkins University Press, 1996).

the developing world will be dominated by concerns about access to energy and mineral resources and about international security.

Vernon W. Ruttan

Foreword

Involuntary poverty is an unmitigated evil. All development efforts aim at eradicating it and enabling all people to develop their full potential. Yet all too often in the process of development it is the poor who shoulder the heaviest burden. It is development itself that interferes with human and cultural development. In the transition from subsistence-oriented agriculture to commercial agriculture, poor women and children are sometimes hit hardest. In the transition from a traditional society, in which the extended family takes care of its members who suffer misfortunes, to a market society, in which the community has not yet taken on responsibility for the victims of the competitive struggle, the fate of these victims can be cruel. In the transition from rural patron-client relationships to relations based on the cash nexus, the poor suffer by losing one type of support without gaining another. In the transition from an agricultural to an industrial society, the public authorities neglect the majority of the rural people in favor of the urban population. In the transitions that we are now witnessing from centrally planned to market-oriented economies, and from autocracies to democracies, inflation, mass unemployment, growing poverty, alienation, and new crimes have to be endured. In spite of four decades of development efforts, poverty remains high in many areas of the world. Over a billion people are estimated to fall below the poverty line.

When I worked with Gunnar Myrdal in the 1960s on *Asian Drama,* he devoted a lot of energy to showing how "inadequate to reality" our conceptual apparatus was: how our concepts, models, theories were biased in a way that advanced our interests. Even ignorance can be opportunistic. Eberhard Reusse quotes with approval Quarles van Ufford: "The survival of development policy and its administration are dependent on sufficient ignorance . . . it greatly encourages to ignore facts about the local level . . . this construction of both knowledge and ignorance provides some sort of stability." The sociology of knowledge or rather of false beliefs and opinions and of ignorance is one of the most interesting parts in this valuable book.

Yet in at least one respect Myrdal himself fell a victim to these Northern or Western biases. He, in the company of many development experts in the 1950s and 1960s, regarded most indigenous cultural factors as obstacles to development. He thought that the people in the developing countries are lethargic and work-shy; lack hygiene; have no desire to make money; lack willingness to cooperate, to experiment, to explore, and to adopt a rational approach; and that their traditional attitudes are hostile to development. In short, that they are not like modern Swedes.

For Myrdal the modern Swedish welfare state was the model for Asia, not cultural autonomy. He was Eurocentric; he did not rejoice in cultural diversity. There is a fundamental difference in his own attitudes in *Asian Drama* from those in *An American Dilemma:* unlike in *American Dilemma,* in *Asian Drama* Myrdal failed to identify with the people. In spite of his emphasis on attitudes and institutions, which he regarded mainly as obstacles and inhibitions to the modernization ideals, he was indifferent or hostile to local tradition, to indigenous art, to the religions of the region.

In Myrdal's view South Asia was largely a poor, unhygienic, corrupt, illiterate, and economically backward region. Yet South Asia and other developing areas are proud of their rich culture. South Asia, for example, is the cradle of some of the greatest civilizations of the world that sprang from the religious traditions of Hinduism, Buddhism, and Islam. It has a rich tradition in art and literature. It is known for its unique flavor of food and music. The region is also known for its significant strides in architecture, astronomy, and medicine. Its ancient traditions of effective governance at the local level are also outstanding.

Although Myrdal was highly critical of the power of the state bureaucracy, there is not much in his book about popular participation. A deep pessimism about development prospects in general and development aid in particular pervades his later work.

The role of culture in development has recently been much discussed and clarified. Most people value goods and services because of what they contribute to our freedom to live the way we value. Culture must be judged beyond its purely instrumental role in contributing to economic growth. What we have reason to value—the court of last appeal—must itself be a matter of culture. Education, for example, promotes economic growth and is therefore of instrumental value, but at the same time it is an essential part of cultural development with intrinsic value. Hence we cannot reduce culture to a subsidiary position as a mere promoter of economic growth.

Since Myrdal's death we have discovered that we have to build on local cultures: both as an end, because cultural diversity is admirable in itself and creative, and as a means to development. But it is undeniable that some traditional cultural features militate against development. Not all features of local culture are desirable or advance development. There is a universal, global ethics that does not tolerate some traditional customs. Neither all tradition nor all modernity is to be welcomed. The repressive nature of both some traditional values and structures and some modern ones is evident. Tradition can spell stagnation, oppression, inertia, privilege; modernization can amount to alienation and a loss of identity and sense of community. The difficult challenge is to build modernity on tradition. Japan has succeeded in combining modernity with tradition. Traditional consumption habits, community loyalties, and cooperative attitudes have contributed, until recently, to the fantastic economic growth of the country.

Eberhard Reusse analyzes with great skill and insight the damage that can be done by imposing Western or European concepts, models, paradigms, prescriptions, and policies on the developing countries. His two case studies demonstrate this damage inflicted by donor-imposed policies. He calls his book "an exercise in provocation." I hope that it will be widely read and that the complacent donor community will be provoked.

Paul Streeten

Preface

This is an exercise in provocation. For the past three decades I have been an advocate of intellectual truth, modesty, and cost/benefit consciousness in development assistance. My necessarily critical input had to be packaged diplomatically. Therefore, I reached only those willing to receive the messages. Today, after a life of active service in the development-assistance machine, I have decided to speak with a louder voice.

In seeking to balance the self-serving success story so often propagated by the aid-channeling establishment, the politically and financially less powerful critique tends to convey an overdose of challenge if not provocation, inviting the retaliatory charge of biased reporting. As observed by a reviewer of Jackson and Eade's *Against the Grain:*

> there is no doubt that [the authors] have gone out of their way to find failures, and have not written a "balanced" account. But neither do the donors provide a balanced view. Instead of repelling [the authors'] assaults, they should re-assess their own rationale for project . . . aid. If the claims they advance for their projects were changed to bear a closer resemblance to reality, critics . . . would have greater difficulty . . . shooting them down in flames. (Stevens 1983, 57)

My acquaintance with individual organizations, programs, and projects influenced the selection of examples. No comparative judgment is intended; similar performances can be found all across the aid-channeling arena. The organization I served the longest, the Food and Agriculture Organization (FAO), naturally features prominently in certain sections. FAO has to be acknowledged for the comparative openness with which critical views are received and discussed, for an intellectually conducive atmosphere that has developed further under its present director general. Although this organization receives more critical analysis here, that does not mean that its paradigms and programs are weaker than others' or that my intention is to criticize the organization. I hope that constructive critique will further the insight that FAO, as a United Nations (UN) specialized agency, may do better by strengthening its role as a source of professional information, evaluation, advice, arbitration, standard setting, and intellectual ferment—in short, as a "centre of excellence"—rather than by competing in the congested donor market for project funds and in the "balkanized" aid-receiving arena for scarce project servicing and counterpart personnel resources.

Much information on case histories was gathered during a brief period of informal research cooperation with FAO for academic purposes, in 1993. I am grateful to the organization for access to published and unpublished material and for staff interviews during this period and on sporadic later visits, as well as to the many former colleagues, too numerous to mention, who assisted with valuable comments on draft chapters, especially with regard to the final recommendations. My grateful acknowledgment is due as well to the German Agency for Technical Cooperation (GTZ) for the opportunity to contribute to several of its recent programs in Africa, especially those related to postharvest systems, grain marketing, and cereal banks.

This study evolved from a discussion of development problems with professors John P. Neelsen and Jürgen H. Wolff at the Ruhr University, Bochum, in 1991. Three decades of experience in development assistance in over forty countries distributed over all developing regions appeared worth condensing and systematizing within the framework of a sociopolitical thesis. My grateful acknowledgment goes especially to Professor Wolff, whose stimulating and constructive tutoring accompanied the undertaking.

The thesis was distributed in Germany in 1999 by the Ruhr University's Institute of Development Research and Policy. After its encouraging reception in Germany, I realized that it would reach a wider market through an internationally known publisher. I am grateful to George Rosen, professor emeritus of the University of Illinois, for recommending this book to the University of Chicago Press for publication.

The present edition takes into account new factual and intellectual elements in the current development debate. The recommendations are more clearly structured than in the first edition and have expanded, especially with regard to a division of roles between governmental and nongovernmental development assistance and the advancement of privatization options for the development community.

The style of the book, including its recommendations, remains provocative. Not all that is easily condemned can as easily be corrected. I have rightly been reminded that political patterns have probably been underrated in my recommendations. Eventually, a workable path to improvement may oscillate around a compromise between technically constructive and politically appeasing solutions. May this book add a pinch of salt to the outcome!

Abbreviations

ACOPAM	Appui cooperative de développement assistée par le Program Alimentative Mondial en zone Soudano-Sahelien (semiautonomous subprogram of ILO), Geneva
AGS	Agricultural Support Systems Division (FAO)
BC	Banque de céréales
BIT	Bureau International du Travail (French title of ILO), Geneva
CB	Cereal bank: synonymous with banque de céréales (BC), grenier de prévoyance (GP), and Getreide Bank (GB)
CILSS	Comité International pour la Lutte contre la Sécheresse au Sahel, Ouagadougou
DANIDA	Danish International Development Agency, Copenhagen
EEC	European Economic Community
FAO	Food and Agriculture Organization of the UN, Rome
FONADES	Fonds National du Développement Economique et Social, Burkina Faso
FOVODES	Fonds Voltaique du Développement Economique et Social (predecessor of FONADES), Upper Volta, now Burkina Faso
GASGA	Group for Assistance on Systems for Grains after Harvest (previously Group for Assistance on Storage of Grain in Africa), secretariat shifting in turn among the member organizations, such as FAO, NRI, and GTZ
GNP	Gross national product
GTZ	Deutsche Gesellschaft für Technische Zusammenarbeit, Eschborn (German Agency for Technical Cooperation)
IDS	Institute of Development Studies, Brighton (Sussex University)
IFAD	International Fund for Agricultural Development, Rome
IGO	International governmental organization
ILO	International Labor Office (see also BIT), Geneva
IMF	International Monetary Fund, Washington, D. C.
LDC	Least-developed countries (48 by UN classification, 70% African)
NGO	Nongovernmental organization
NRI	Natural Resources Institute, Chatham Maritime (previously TPI)
ODA	Official development assistance
OECD	Organization for Economic Cooperation and Development, Paris

Oxfam	Oxford Committee on Famine Relief, Oxford
PBE	Division of Program, Budget and Evaluation (FAO), Rome
PBEE	PBE, Evaluation Service
PFL	Prevention of Food Losses (FAO/SAP)
PRMC	Program pour la Restructuration des Marchés Céréaliers, Mali
SAP	Special action program
SNV	Stifting Nederlandse Vrÿvilligers, The Hague
SOFA	"The State of Food and Agriculture" (annual review, by FAO)
TPI	Tropical Products Institute (now NRI), formerly at Slough
UN	United Nations
UNDP	United Nations Development Program, New York
USAID	United States Agency for International Development, Washington, D.C.
VENRO	Verband Entwicklungspolitik deutscher Nicht-Regierungsorganisationen (association of German development NGOs), Bonn
WFP	World Food Program, Rome

Introduction

Development discourse long ago lost its optimism. Now that formerly affluent governments in traditional donor countries are facing political battles for tax increases of only one-tenth percent, public support for Third World development aid of up to 5% of disposable household income begins to falter. Voices calling for scaling down and even phasing out development aid[1] are gaining strength. Third World countries are realizing that aid imports dependency and crowds out the development of sustainable government structures. Some are gaining the courage to refuse further "development" loans, which in the past too often have produced little lasting effect other than long-term indebtedness.

In this situation, the present study aims to analyze the aid pathology, to identify causes and effects, and to arrive at an explanatory model as a constructive contribution to the evolution of a new intellectual policy environment.

The study has four chapters. Chapter 1 is an academic excursion orbiting the "development" paradigm, subjecting it to a variety of often provocative viewpoints in relation to "globalization," "culture," "bureaucracy," "rhetoric," "episteme," and "theory," while aiming to unbalance stereotypes, casting doubt on previous convictions and demonstrating a broad range of possible interpretations of real or imagined phenomena. Chapter 2 describes two case studies, which permit an insight into the day-to-day running of the "development" machine and serve as a reference pool for diagnostic analysis. Chapter 3 is a structured analysis and discussion of the principal components of the aid pathology, from behavioral, environmental, and cognitive perspectives, drawing on the case studies, the author's overall work experience, and the experiences and analyses of other authors. Chapter 4 presents conclusions, based on the interaction model derived in chapter 3, and therapeutic recommendations.

To readers less interested in academic discourse and the details of a case study, chapters 3 (analysis and discussion) and 4 (conclusions and recommendations) provide the essential arguments and messages of the study.

---

1. See, e.g., Elliot Berg, "Whither Aid to Africa?" Dublin Talk for Aid Advisory Committee, June 1997.

Chapter 1

The Background

1.1   Thinking about Development

The following excursion into academic discourse around selected topics of
relevance to the hypothetical challenge of this study is not meant to be representative; neither does it aim at considered value statements or conclusions.
While the overall picture emerging is heterogeneous, an undercurrent of skep-
ticism, critical analysis, and rebellion vis-à-vis the commonplace rhetoric
governing the development community is discernible.

The discussion is subdivided into seven topics: (1) the impasse of development theory; (2) the "march of paradigms"; (3) Kuhn, epistemic communities,
and the "interventionist paradigm"; (4) the rhetoric of development; (5) organizations, institutions, and development bureaucracies; (6) development and
culture; and (7) development and globalization.

The treatment of these topics is aphoristic, using ample direct quotations
from relevant publications. Some topics, notably 3, 5, and 6, are featured more
extensively than might be expected from a background chapter. However,
though less exposed to public limelight than other spheres in the aid arena,
these topics get to the heart of the aid dilemma. The reader is therefore invited
to be tolerant toward some more elaborate excursions through frequently diverging viewpoints in these pages.

1.1.1   The Impasse of Development Theory

Theory makes reality transparent, illuminates structures, trends, causalities; it
opens comprehensive conceptualization, for example, the deduction of the
concept "forest" from the visual apprehension of numerous trees (Marx 1972,
12). Theory is useful to the extent that such comprehension is facilitated, that
is, that its application provides "Verstehenshilfe" (ibid.).

The once dominant ("hegemonic," van Donge 1995, 282) development
theories have become redundant in this regard. Their major assumptions have
become untenable. "Three major biases" were revealed: "a teleological bias
which sees social change as directed towards a universal path of development;
a functional bias which assumes that development necessarily sustains particular world orders; and centralism, as social change is depicted as emanating
from the centre" (283).

"The object of the world system has been transformed so radically since the
late 60s that it has begun to resist the conventional narratives of the discipline"
(Corbridge 1990, 623). Consequently, development analysts deplore "a
knowledge and theory deficit" in an environment where "change, politics and

cross-cultural relations are inherently complex and riddled with dilemmas for which there are seldom simple satisfactory answers" (Tisch and Wallace 1994, summarized by Knop 1995, 353), where decentralized and multilineal processes dominate (Newitt 1995, cited in van Donge 1995, 282).

As a result, "development" as a self-explanatory target is no longer convincing. "Along with 'anti-development' and 'beyond development,' postdevelopment (rejecting development) is a radical reaction to the dilemmas of development" (Nederveen-Pieterse 2000, 175). In 1992 already, Krugman observed: "Once upon a time there was a field called development economics . . . That field no longer exists" (2); and Sachs (1992, 1) concluded: "The idea of development stands like a ruin in the intellectual landscape." In the meantime "theoretical chaos" (Aurois 1995, 120) prevails.

Interpretative sociology is called to help, where "theory is not used to 'predict' but is employed in dialogue with evidence" in order to "reveal tendencies in human behavior which can manifest themselves in many ways, and in this way development theory can move away from the determinism which the assumed outcome of particular order presumes" (van Donge 1995, 283, summarizing Vandergeest and Buttel 1988, 688).

Both Long and van der Ploeg's "actor-oriented analysis" (1989, 226), which views development intervention as a "multiple reality made up of differing cultural perceptions and social interests," and Ruttan and Hayami (1984) in their endogenously induced model for agricultural institutions and technologies signify the departure from simplistic interventionist development concepts. The final disconnection of development processes from human planning and control seems to be embodied in Luhmann's theorem (1984, 1992) of the autopoietic reproduction of social systems (Scherr 1995, 148–49) and in "sociology's institutionalism" with its claim of "powerful evidence of global cultural homogenization," contesting the "myth" of bureaucratic rationality (Finnemore 1996, 328–30).

Against the background of dwindling resources for sustained global economic growth, "development" may also be defined as "a society's sustainable response/adaptation[1] to changes in its socio-economic and/or natural environment," including the invasion of commercial, technical, and cultural innovations, to which the response might be whole or partial acceptance, rejection, exploitation, conversion, or adaptation (Reusse 1993, 466). "A new morality based on self-restraint is put forward by the adherents of the risk society . . . Having entered the twenty-first century the notion of progress [or "growth"] seems to have lost much of its hegemonic status within development studies" (Schuurman 2000, 16).

---

1. The emphasis on adaptation, often requiring innovative capacity, as the essence of development is not new and was already present in Toynbee's challenge/response paradigm (1961). In the social sciences Coleman (1971), Costello (1994, 349), and Huntington (1979), among others, gave "adaptation" central importance, as does New Institutional Economics (North 1994).

1.1.2   The March of Paradigms

As development theories went out of fashion, "paradigms" came "marching in."[2] Indeed, since Kuhn's influential work, *The Structure of Scientific Revolutions* (1962), in which he gives the paradigm prominence in his analysis of the evolution of the natural sciences, the term gradually invaded the human sciences also, particularly the social sciences. It serves to package any school of thought that seeks to be recognized as relevant to scientific or professional debate, without the commitment to solidity, comprehensive structure, and interdependencies expected of theory. Whereas a new theory requires a high degree of maturity in order to survive the academic battle that its arrival will predictably provoke,[3] "a paradigm is at the start largely a promise of success discoverable in selected and still incomplete examples" (Kuhn 1962, 23). "What is taking place today in development studies, is a theoretical disruption, a standstill in the formulation of theories, as well as a very likely appearance or creation of a number of paradigms" (Aurois 1995, 120).

Though "within development studies it was always difficult to separate theories from paradigms because of its strong normative orientation," the character of the debates within the discipline now clearly seems to "have shifted from theory to paradigm" (Schuurman 2000, 8, 13). As a jack-of-all-trades, "paradigm" has become an "in-word" covering an ever widening range of meanings, for example:

- *Interchangeable and quasi-synonymous with "theory"* and vice versa, cf. van Donge (1995, 282): "neither the modernization nor the dependency paradigms could come to terms with diverse outcomes in development."
- Referring to *dismissed or invalidated theories or premises,* cf. Finnemore (1996, 328), who argues that sociology's institutionalism reveals "features of international politics assumed away by other paradigms" and disempowers "issues that are assumed rather than investigated by our dominant paradigms"; and Shimomura (1995, 363) reviewing Carlsson et al. 1994: "The authors reject the so-called rational paradigm of organization."
- Serving as *a demonstrative example,* cf. Lumsdaine (1993, 29), quoted in Krueger 1995, 671: "foreign aid is a paradigm case of the influence of crucial moral principle because of its universal scope, as assistance from well-off nations to any in need."
- *Model/concept,* cf. Knop (1995, 354), summarizing Tisch and Wallace 1994: "depending on how the new world order will shake out there will probably be more activity based in paradigms that are alternative to the now-dominant Western model."

---

2. Streeten (1995a, 210), fatigued by the "march of paradigms," especially the "alleged new ones."

3. "Theorie ist ein umstrittenes Gebiet, das man nur hinreichend gerüstet betreten sollte" (Marx 1972, 13).

- *Viewpoint/message,* cf. Schwab (1995, 567) reviewing Widner 1994: "These two essays . . . lay out the essential paradigm of the book."
- *A worldview,* cf. Streeten (1995a, 210), reviewing Naqvi 1993: "he interprets 'paradigm' broadly as a distinct Weltanschauung."
- *An often ideologically loaded program,* cf. Sanyal (1994, 33): "The AD [alternative development] paradigm was primarily concerned with equity and redistributional issues . . . direct attack on poverty . . . meeting basic human needs"; Najam (1996, 447): "a new paradigm of relationships may need to be put in place . . . paradigm where both [donor and beneficiary] are patrons and clients simultaneously"; Pretty and Chambers (1993, 2): "These paradigmatic approaches . . . the components of the new paradigm imply a new professionalism"; and Chambers (1993, 276): "The prescriptive paradigm of reversals for rural development . . . near the core of the paradigm is decentralized process and choice."
- *An image of reality biased toward a justification for intervention: the "interventionist paradigm"* (for further explanation see section 1.1.3).

1.1.3   Kuhn, Epistemic Communities, and the Interventionist Paradigm

A mutually supportive relationship is at work between a paradigm and a scientific or professional elite (epistemic community) that subscribes to it. Kuhn's 1962 influential work supplied basic inputs for the study of epistemic communities. P. M. Haas (1997, 3), one of the pioneers in the integration of the epistemic-community phenomenon in the study of international organizations, likens the phenomenon (a "thought collective . . . a sociological group with a common style of thinking") to "Kuhn's broader social definition of a paradigm, which is an entire constellation of beliefs, values, techniques, and so on shared by members of a given community and which governs not a subject matter but a group of practitioners." In Haas's own definition, "an epistemic community is a network of professionals with recognized expertise and competence in a particular domain and an authoritative claim to policy-relevant knowledge within that domain or issue area" (ibid.). Much earlier, Ruggie (1975, 569–70), borrowing the term "episteme" from Foucault, had introduced the "knowledge" dilemma, defining episteme as "a dominant way of looking at social reality, a set of shared symbols and references, mutual expectations and mutual predictability of intention . . . Epistemic communities may be said to consist of interrelated roles which grow up around an episteme; they delimit, for their members, *the* proper construction of social reality."

Kuhn (1962) had already alluded to the risk of yielding development deficits through misguided epistemes supported by complacent or self-centered epistemic communities: "one of the things a community acquires with a paradigm is a criterion for choosing problems that, while the paradigm is taken for granted, can be assumed to have solutions . . . other problems . . . are rejected . . . A paradigm can, for that matter, even insulate the community from those socially important problems that are not reducible to the puzzle form, because they cannot be stated in terms of the conceptual and instrumental tools the paradigm implies" (37).[4] Efforts to verify a paradigm are characterized as "attempts to force nature into the preformed and relatively inflexible box that the paradigm supplies" (24). P. M. Haas (1997, 23) dwells extensively on these risks, especially where "the epistemological impossibility of confirming access to reality means that the group responsible for articulating the dimensions of reality has great social and political influence . . . [and] can identify and represent what is of public concern, particularly in cases in which the physical manifestations of a problem are themselves unclear." In the same vein, M. Haas (1992, 250), with particular reference to social science paradigms, speaks of "conflicting paradigms" that "distort a barely knowable reality in accordance with ideological preferences."

Subjectivity is nearly always involved. According to Kuhn (1962, 4), "an apparently arbitrary element, compounded of personal and historical accident, is always a formative ingredient of the beliefs espoused by a given scientific community at a given time." Equally relevant is the risk of corrupt or opportunistic use of the authority entrusted to, or usurped by, an epistemic community. Examples given by Finnemore (1993, 570), P. M. Haas (1997, 11, 24), Toye (1991), and Tvedt (1998, 146, 193, 215) point to the influence of funding and career-advancement opportunities on the direction of policy advice given by specialist communities.

Epistemic communities often initiate and/or facilitate an interventionist paradigm, that is, a construction of reality biased toward proving a justification for intervention of a kind that makes use of a community's specialization. In the aid world those paradigms are nearly always welcomed by donors, technical-assistance agencies, and nongovernmental organizations (NGOs) eager to employ (releasing, channeling, or attracting) aid funds in cash or kind. Finnemore (1996) provides a thorough analysis of an international governmental organization (IGO) that superimposed on its member states a standard institutional innovation promoted by its professional clique.

A paradigm leading to planned intervention[5] strengthens the reputation, self-esteem, fund-channeling and policy-directing influence, and bureaucratic leverage of the professional group or epistemic community that established or pioneered the paradigm. Such interventionist paradigms have been flooding the donor-funds market, feeding the growth of a "techno-managerial elite," which has been condemned as the "New Class" by a counterrebellious sociopolitical movement in the United States.[6] The role of benefactor and interna-

---

4. Naudet (2000) gives central importance to this phenomenon in his analysis of aid history in the Sahel.

5. Defined by Roeling (1988, 39) as "a systematic effort to strategically apply resources to manipulate seemingly causal elements in an ongoing social process, so as to permanently reorient that process in directions deemed desirable by the intervening party."

6. On the "New Class" phenomenon see Ehrenreich 1989, chapter 4.

tional tutor allegedly assumed by this class provoked cynical comments, such as

> Needs assessment is the worst kind of artificial negativity created by the New Class, whereby people are supposed to believe that they are all alike in having "basic human needs," that there are always more needs than can be met, and that only the New Class can help them to meet those needs that can be met. It would seem that the techno-managerial elite alone has the diagnostic credentials to manage the therapeutic society. (Roe 1995a, 158)

> [N]eeds became an important emblem which allowed managers to provide a philanthropic rationale for the destruction of cultures [as well as] the most appropriate term to designate the moral relations between strangers in a dreamt of world made up of well-fare states. (Illich 1992, 98–99)

This rebellion against the New Class regime is probably coupled with an aversion to the self-confidence of a complacent academe at being "*the* source of cognitive authority."[7] Development management categories such as resources, basic needs, and participation are judged as an "ultimately self-serving and reinforcing creation of the experts," while "communities do not 'need' outside experts to manage their resources" (Roe 1995a, 159). In this context the provocative argument of no less a proponent of this populist philosophy than Michel Foucault may be quoted, that is, that "the masses do not need intellectuals to understand things; they have a complete, clear and better knowledge than intellectuals and are well able to express it" (Foucault and Deleuze 1987, 107).[8]

1.1.4   The Rhetoric of Development

The ponderous jargon of much routine development discourse, especially that contained in conference, publicity, and official policy documents, has been widely recognized and commented on. The criticism of the New Class rhetoric outlined above also highlights this aspect. In "a largely successful attempt to deconstruct . . . current buzzwords," such as "participation" or "equity," an analysis by Moore and Schmitz (1995) "strives to show how the language of development has been captured and deprived of any meaningful content by development elites" (Kiely 1996, 959).

Watts (1986, 377), reviewing Gunilla and Beckmann's 1985 account of the role of wheat bread in Nigeria, sharply criticizes the use of the word "crisis" in

---

7. Barnes and Edge 1982, 2: "In modern societies, science is near to being *the* source of cognitive authority: anyone who would be widely believed and trusted as an interpreter of nature needs a license from the scientific community."

8. Author's translation from the German.

development jargon, especially "crisis in agriculture" in Africa: "In spite of the complex picture of the myriads of diverse African farming systems that has been painted by recent research, the lexicon of *'general crisis'* has entered popular and professional discourse almost without critique. Yet the crisis vernacular obfuscates both the details of local agricultural performance and indeed clouds the object of study itself." In like manner, Jiggins, Reijntjes, and Lightfoot (1996), and before them Jaeger (1992), effectively dismantle the "general African food crisis" paradigm by proving that the importance of the cereal component in African consumption and production systems has been overemphasized, though little understood, by developers.[9]

Long and van der Ploeg (1989, 231) speak of development intervention as "involving a kind of 'trade in images,' " whose construction is sustained by a "process of labeling which functions to promote or impose certain interpretive schemata concerned with the diagnosis and solution of 'development problems.' " Roe (1995b, 1066) concludes: "[T]he more crisis narratives generated by an expert elite, the more the elite appears to have established a claim to the resources it says are subject to crisis."

This drive for a standardized, "labeled" approach to the identification of development "needs" is well summarized by Chambers (1993, 260): "Aid agencies with large budgets, especially the banks, need packages to promote. Academics need ideologies to dissect and denounce. Institutions and their members need and seek shared values and concepts to sustain solidarity . . . and all these need a common language and set of concerns for dialogue and debate, for securing and legitimating flows of funds, and as a framework for thought and action."[10] The result often resembles a self-referential "perpetuum mobile," floating on its ritual oratory, but prompting an unimpressed observer to comment: "By making every issue a global issue, the United Nations is attempting to create a world that does not exist" (Helms 1996, 5).

---

9. "The widely held view that Africa suffers from a chronic food crisis lacks clear empirical support. Apart from suggesting that removing policy distortions could ameliorate Africa's food situation, the findings here do not lead to more specific policy implications. What they do suggest, however, is that a course of action based on the belief that Africa has lost the capacity to feed itself will be misguided" (Jaeger 1992, 642).

10. "The NGOs mushrooming in the developing countries do not necessarily express societal needs and values in a particular country, but mirror needs and values expressed at UN conferences, donor conferences, etc. . . . The actors basically learn and rhetorically internalize the same language and 'symbolic orders' as they are socialized in the channel's routinized practices [exploiting] an 'image monopoly' in portraying the poorest among the poor and their development needs in Western donor countries" (Tvedt 1998, 65, 77, 78).

1.1.5   Organizations, Institutions, and Development Bureaucracies

> History shows that wherever bureaucracy gained the upper
> hand . . . it did not disappear again unless in the course of
> the total collapse of the supporting culture.
>
> Max Weber

Even Max Weber, in his earlier works the acknowledged advocate of the "rational" paradigm of formal bureaucratic institutions, created and controlled by their founders as efficient and obedient instruments in the administration of modern society,[11] lost faith in the manageability of these "robot" creations. Despite the schools of functionalism and new institutional economics, rational interpretation of institutionalization has been losing ground. Luhmann's theorem of autopoietic systems (1984) and Meyer and Rowan's challenge (1977) to the rational model by what today is labeled "sociology's institutionalism" (Finnemore 1996, 325) have supplied paradigms of self-referential institutional entities within a universal institutional ecology.

The basic argument of sociology's institutionalism is that "external cultural legitimation rather than task demands or functional needs explains much if not most of organizational behaviour" (Finnemore 1996, 330). This cultural legitimation is seen as particularly obvious in multilateralism with its mushroomed population of international organizations.[12] "Attributes or behaviour of the units correlate with attributes and behaviour of other units or with worldwide phenomena (international conferences, historical events)" rather than with specific task demands: "participation in the growing network of IGOs is culturally necessary and 'appropriate.' . . . the picture painted by institutionalist studies is one in which the world culture marches effortless and faceless across the globe" (338–39).

Shanks, Jacobson, and Kaplan (1996, 593 ff.)[13] speak of the "IGO population" as part of organizational populations that, like biological populations, acquire dynamic properties that affect their development. They have learned to "cling like a barnacle to its niche" and, need or opportunity arising, "spawn" new IGOs (their "emanations").[14] The older an IGO or any governmental organization is, the greater its chance of surviving in the organizational ecology.

---

11. "Designed to induce an impersonal and rational orientation towards tasks which is conducive to efficient administration" (Narayana 1992, 124).

12. The *Yearbook of International Organizations* (2000–2001), updated annually by the Union of International Organizations, lists 5,170 intergovermental (up from 1,700 in 1993) and 24,326 international nongovernmental organizations. Obviously, the "age of organization" (Wolin 1960, 352) has still not passed its peak.

13. Shanks, Jacobson, and Kaplan acknowledge borrowing from Hannan and Freeman 1989, Pfeffer 1982, and Scott 1992.

14. E.g., the FAO "spawned the European Commission for Agriculture as well as about 20 other agencies" (Shanks, Jacobson, and Kaplan 1996, 599).

This biological IGO metaphor must not obscure the fact that organizations are run, controlled, and supported by human beings whose interactions are the driving force behind the seemingly autonomous "dynamics" and structural metamorphoses. Shanks, Jacobson, and Kaplan (1996, 593) mention the "constituency" that each organization's presence creates, which, even if realizing the organization's redundancy, would rather let it "slide into obscurity than expand resources in a battle to kill" it. New institutional economics[15] stresses "path dependence," for example, referring to the NGO sector ("complex agencies under pressure in transitional processes in which control of resource allocation is shifting from one group to another"): "The very creation of an NGO as an institution involves processes that will work against its dissolution" (Cameron 2000, 632–33).

Crozier (1963), Bourdieu (1977), Mintzberg (1979), as well as Mayer, Stevenson, and Webster (1985), among others, have analyzed the human battlefield ("arena") in and around organizations. Progressive professionalization, especially in IGOs, and the growing intra- and interorganizational silent power of epistemic communities have become the object of social-scientific analysis. The latter "can insinuate their views and influence governments (and IGOs) by occupying niches in advisory and regulatory bodies" (P. M. Haas 1997, 30). They can prove particularly influential in policy coordination. Since "governments and organizations may be said to learn through the evolution of consensual knowledge," epistemic communities as transmitters of this knowledge can become very powerful indeed. As an "invisible college" cutting across the organizations, they can "play an important role in integrating the fragmented IGO programme" (ibid.).

However, Haas continues, explaining organizations' phlegmatic responsiveness to needs for adaptation, "once in place, a group will persist until subsequent crisis challenges its ability to provide advice." "In the absence of crisis, there will be little reconsideration of choices."[16] Mayntz (1992, 28), among others, has analyzed the political influence of interorganizational networks, for example, as a consensual bloc impeding or moderating change. While recognizing the "embeddedness of states in an international social system" and the role for IGOs "as an arena in which norms and convergent expectations about international behavior are developed," Finnemore (1993, 570–71), in her United Nations Education, Scientific, and Cultural Organization (UNESCO) example, shows how international communities of experts can use IGOs "as a base from which to wield influence," motivated more by bureaucratic ambitions than by "professional norms in the science community or principled beliefs about science."

---

15. Following North (1990), this economic approach interprets "institutions" as "rules of behavior—ways of doing things that structure human interaction. Organizations are the players and interact with the institutions, each influencing the other" (Meyer 1995, 1281).

16. P. M. Haas (1997, 34), referring to Blau's "elasticity of demand for advice" (1967).

Opportunism, lobbyism, and free-riding are common motivations driving actors in and around organizations, be they government organizations, IGOs, NGOs, or international NGOs. One of the paradigms that enhances our understanding of the popularity of IGOs is consociationalism. According to Taylor (1993, quoted in Brewin 1994, 267), under it "inward-looking communities may safeguard their separate identities where a cartel of their elites can reach agreement among themselves by consensus in institutions where there is representation in proportion to the relative powers of the communities they represent." Brewin applies the paradigm to the European Community, whose members take advantage of a "semi-detached life of nations on the common European estate," quoting John Major's famous claim of May 1993: "There is only one aim at the heart of our European policy: the cold calculation of Britain's national interest" (ibid.).

Addressing the growing ambition of NGOs, both northern and southern, to include entrepreneurial orientations in their growth and survival strategies, a new institutional economist (Meyer 1995, 1277) ventured this paradigm: "entrepreneurial economic entities producing international public goods" within a theoretical framework that assumes "self-interested behaviour coexisting with loyalty, commitment and altruism as well as opportunism." His subsequent case studies, however, arrive at the conclusion that "economic entrepreneurship is a powerful side of NGOs, neglected in popular vision inspired by the grassroots and political action. Clearly, strong relationships with governments, the for-profit sector, and international donors alter the incentives that nonprofit NGOs face . . . the allocation of benefits . . . cannot be expected to be either optimal or egalitarian" (1285).[17]

Finally, the paradigm based on the "theory of artificial negativity" (Roe 1995a, 149) argues that "the techno-managerial elite fosters artificial negativity" (bureaucracies engendering counterbureaucracies), "which in the beginning gives the appearance of opposition, in the process supports the elite, and in the end leads to more and more bureaucratic involution."[18] This model is not inapplicable to some NGOs, which from initial "rebels" soon developed into additional middlemen in the distribution channel for official development assistance (ODA). Populist critique, with reference to this kind of artificial negativity in the "sustainable development" debate, for example, insists that

---

17. "Full decentralization based on cooperatives, voluntary organizations, non-profit structures and NGOs, which I would call the populist utopia, has had an increasing influence in the global debate in many countries. However, historical analysis of the costs and benefits of the visible and invisible hands may prove to be an interesting exercise for future scholars" (Simai 1996, 25).

18. "Involution": a kind of bureaucratic infarct; a practically unmanageable situation of bureaucratic entanglement; regulations and counterregulations creating administrative dilemmas whose solution calls for ever more regulations; politically, involution threatens consensus-abiding lobby-camp democracy (consensual bloc impeding action for necessary adaptation; cf. Mayntz 1992).

"what is really going on in this so-called controversy is New Class experts jockeying among themselves in claiming stewardship over land and resources they do not own" (Roe 1995a, 159).

A veteran analyst of the "civil society" paradigm refers to the problematic legitimacy claimed by activists from northern NGOs in the development arena: "Who do these people represent? . . . Chasing development funds from those they seek to influence[19] and not particularly concerned with internal democracy," they seem "poorly equipped to meet that challenge of legitimacy" (van Rooy 2000, 314).

1.1.6   Development and Culture

> It is much easier to construct factories, bridges, stadiums, etc. using foreign aid technicians than to change the cognitive map (socio-economic way of life, attitude, beliefs, values, etc.) of the rural farming community.
>
> Gunnar Myrdal

Development economists, influenced by Max Weber's 1905 classic and the wide-angle approach of the new institutional economics school, try to incorporate "cultural variables into a baseline economic growth model" (Granato, Inglehart, and Leblang 1996, 607). They conclude that cultural and economic arguments should be integrated in a complementary way in future theoretical and empirical work (626). Culture, defined as "a system of basic common values that help shape the behavior of people in a given society" (608), is analyzed in terms of its influence on saving and achievement motivation. Preindustrial societies are dismissed as "zero-sum systems . . . hostile to social mobility and individual economic accumulation" (607–8). The Weberian era of growth through individual economic accumulation is seen as superseded by a postmaterialist shift in values in much of Western industrialized society that "could be viewed as the erosion of the Protestant Ethic among populations that experience high levels of economic security" (609). Once the new values become widespread, economic growth is assumed to slow down or disappear.

The question is whether the idea of "development," even in a purely economic definition, needs to remain predominantly centered on the material growth factor expressed in rising per capita income. Under ecological constraints, may it not already be an achievement for a society to accommodate natural population growth at a stable per capita income, or, by way of sustainable adaptation to endo- and exogenous changes, to secure optimal stability by

---

19. Symptomatic is the remark by a member of the European Commission (EC) in Brussels, referring to the conspicuous NGO lobby for European Economic Community (EEC) development funds: "It looks as if NGOs act only around EC buildings" (VENRO 1998, 19).

accepting a reduced material per capita consumption, not excluding the substitution of immaterial for material need satisfaction?[20]

Bierschenk and Elwert (1991, 25) warn against studying the cultures of simple people ("einfache Leute") only as survival systems, for this ignores their creativity and inherent dynamism. Their empirical research concludes that most "project" interventions based on simplistic paradigms of "poverty" and "innovation" tend to block autonomous, selectively differentiated, innovative ingenuity through the massive dominance of the standardized prescriptive (and mostly inappropriate) "development" inputs by the administration. Much earlier, Roberts (1975, 50) emphasized the individualist creativity of African farmers and the inappropriateness of standardized agricultural-input supply packages in small-farmer credit schemes: "Neither credit institutions, nor those directing their policies, are as well placed as the farmer to make a decision on his individual investment strategy."

The history of administered "development" blunders in misconception and depreciation of local culture (in the definition quoted above) is well documented. Behnke (1994, 5–6) points out that African pastoralism has "long practiced the 'opportunistic' forms of resource exploitation which were previously condemned but are now endorsed by scientific ecology." Given our "collective inexperience," he advises that "the accumulated experience of pastoral communities may provide our most reliable guide for the redesign of African range management policy," including "institutional arrangements" (ownership, control over resources, etc.). He refers explicitly to the aid lobby's horror scenario of "overstocking" and "desertification," "as these phenomena are not general enough to provide a framework for the formulation of natural resource management policy as a whole." Grazing systems "characterized by complexity, high variability and uncertainty" require "management in the sense of adaptive coping, rather than optimization and control" (8).

Warner (1991, 53), in a paper for FAO on resource management in the human tropics, analyzes the virtues of shifting cultivation and concludes: "The very reason that swiddeners succeed is by accepting the tropical ecosystem and making it work for them. Rather than attempting to 'conquer' [it], the swiddener chooses to manipulate the natural processes of the tropical ecosystem so that it pulses through a stage that is highly productive for him as it returns to forest."

The "very static (Western) approach to the understanding of traditional African agriculture," treating it as a "disrupted equilibrial system that needs readjustment," is seen by Niemeijer (1996, 87) as another "inappropriate paradigm." "It is very likely that the agro-ecosystem in large parts of Africa functions mainly as non-equilibrial (unstable), but nevertheless persistent system in which agriculturists are not inert, but respond in innovative and

---

20. A trend of thought in this direction is met in Ruttan's presentation of "sustainability scenarios," notably the one put forward by the Stockholm Environmental Institute (Ruttan 1999, 2).

dynamic ways to the perturbations of their natural and social environment" (ibid.).

Walker (1995, 164) describes how Western economic assumptions and ecological simplifications got in the way of understanding Somali societies, "favoring sedentary living, though the Somali desert did not." "Time after time, they refused to admit pastoralists' real contributions to the Somali economy," perpetuating their biased assumptions against communal ownership, nomadic pastoralism, and traditional institutions, all three of which proved incorrect. " 'Outmoded' traditional institutions proved far more able to adapt to changing circumstances than the ever-crumbling political institutions imposed from without" (ibid.). "The view from the bottom—of a society that is vigorous, opportunistic and aggressive—is totally different from that at the top, where, in the minds of Somali administrators and foreign development agents, the pastoralist is desperately poor, lethargic, and helpless. Tragically, it is the 'helpless' view that the world sees, and the only one it will respond to" (Gunn 1990, 147).[21] An extensive analysis by Pottier (1996) of the international emergency program for Rwanda after its 1994 civil war reaches similar conclusions. Supported by "disaster-image reinforcing media distortions" (63), "downplaying the existence of effective self-help strategies and the importance of refugee-host relations" and "ignoring the knowledge that is available," a Food and Agriculture Organization and World Food Program (FAO/WFP) "needs" assessment "on the basis of the self-enclosed logic of bureaucracy" (57) paved the way for "outside agencies" to "formulate their own (standardized) version of events and offer their own standardized rescue package" (73).

It pays to acquire an understanding of local culture before applying an interventionist paradigm, because, for development efforts to be successful, "they must be situated within the cultural context" (Geddes, Hughes, and Remenyi 1994, 5). Traditions for mobilizing work parties and maintaining socially vital reciprocity and redistribution systems within a frame of tribal ethics that favorably compare with those prevailing in the "developed world" are reported by a World Bank discussion paper (Shanmugaratnam et al. 1992) on pastoral institutions in the West African Sahel. Project efforts to reduce harvesting and threshing losses in an African rice-growing area remained paradigmatic until project workers identified rational but culture-based variations in local methods, depending on farmland (nature and size), composition of work teams (age group and gender), and relationship with the owner.[22] Taking those culture-specific variations into account drastically reduced the assumed scope for "improvement," but facilitated a more realistic approach.

---

21. For a substantiated view from the bottom that saved the country's robust livestock trading sector from a prospective deprivatization project that might have been financed by the World Bank, see Reusse 1982.

22. "Socio-economic Factors Affecting Post-harvest crop Losses," Parcival Socio-Economic Consulting Services, Sierra Leone, 1985, 8–10.

Uninformed bias, however, is still common in judging rural trading systems. Thus, without further investigation, surprise is expressed in the same consultant report (7) at private traders' paying a farm price of 25% above the official (government-fixed) price. This is seen as "particularly significant because the petty traders usually intervene and buy at lower farm gate prices and make exorbitant profits." Such a sweeping, unsubstantiated statement indicates the presumption and prejudice still present after decades of exposure to trader-averse "grassroots development" ideologies.

Like a fresh breeze, the appeal by Jean H. Guilmette in his address as director of the Club du Sahel challenged encrusted epistemes:[23] "to blow away the webs spun by our myths, to break free of the bonds forged by our thinking"; "to introduce more sober, less dogmatic ideas," "an end to absolute certainties"; and "to exercise patience and . . . prudence" in our work, in the light of a review of the 1980s pointing to "the fact that numerous transplants from outside have been rejected by Sahelian societies because they do not correspond to the cultural realities of the region."

1.1.7   Development and Globalization

The turn of the century has been marked by an ever accelerating globalization process. "Openness denotes internationalization and liberalization of commodity markets, factor markets, and financial markets. Today there is hardly a national economy or company that can afford to ignore international dependencies" (Lang and Ohr 1996, vii). As the factor-price equalization theorem predicts, "convergence," in "unambiguous positive correlation" with globalization (Williamson 1996, 277), has begun to erode the conventional categories of rich and poor, central and peripheral, developed and backward societies. The "world system" has become polycentric and dynamic in a complex, multidimensional process of adaptation to new opportunities and challenges. "International comparative advantage is now liable to shift more rapidly and unexpectedly than in the past; it has become 'kaleidoscopic' " (OECD 1996, 67).

Worldwide economic growth should be a logical consequence of these processes, if the global resources situation did not foreshadow conflicts of sustainability. Under such conditions, there is "a growing need for a long-term vision of the global development process and its various alternatives, in an international world with strong forces of universalism and conformity" (Simai 1996, 35). The "growth" doctrine pervading the "historical drama of transformation and modernization" (ibid., 39) is being superseded by the call of the new institutional economists for "a dynamic theory of social change and an understanding of adaptive efficiency" (North 1994, 5).

Regarding change in the global political structure, Streeten (1995b, 90) considers "four possible developments": "a Utopian global scenario, an oligarchic scenario, a block scenario, and . . . global Balkanization." Change brings

---

23. *Club du Sahel Newsletter,* no. 9, December 1990, cover page.

insecurity and fear. Doomsday theories proliferate, with the risk of triggering reactionary political decisions. While some prophesy the collapse of the "Western capitalist civilization" which, increasingly "maladaptive[,] . . . is rapidly running out of time" (Sanderson 1995, 380; similarly Rich 1994, 164), others predict the usurpation of the "world system" control by a "new historic bloc of transnational interests, including capitalists, sections of the managerial and skilled labor force, the military and cultural elites" (Wilkin 1996, 236).

> [This] emergent transnational class that is inherent within the structured pluralist approach to globalization [will graft itself onto a world system that will be] an integrated totality of social relations . . . [accommodating an] increased integration of production over time and space . . . [accompanied by] . . . the resurgence of infectious diseases, the massive increase in inequality, homelessness, mass migration, hunger and poverty . . . [and] the spread of hyper-rich global cities in which the heights of wealth and power rest alongside the new hyper-exploited. (236)

However, the same author refers to the competitive advantages hitherto enjoyed by the larger (mostly transnational) corporations under inward-looking national development policies granting "subsidies for private profit through tax incentives, enterprise zones, state investment in corporate research and development."[24] He also admits that, therefore, "corporations actually are in favour of state intervention in the economy and always have been" (234). Since "openness" and the harmonization of national economic policies, which thus far have characterized the globalization process, weaken the potential for anticompetitive allocation of state support, transnational corporations' profitability will come under pressure and their performance will be scrutinized by the rules of liberalized global markets.

Development aid in the conventional sense of benevolent resource transfer from donor to receiver countries will lose its importance. Convergence has already become obvious, signaled by rising poverty, unemployment, sclerosis of social services in traditional "donor" societies, and rising real-wage levels in traditional "receiver" societies. National contributions to development assistance and food-aid funds are shrinking.[25] Public "aid fatigue" is spreading. Economic development, in the sense of global factor-cost convergence driven by market incentives, will be more than ever the concern of private entre-

---

24. One may well add, especially for Third World countries, exchange rate, import, and franchise privileges; protective quality and price-control systems; and preferential access to regulated financial markets.

25. The only substantive reference to development assistance (i.e., beyond a somewhat stereotypical food-production concern) in the OECD's 1996 comprehensive policy paper's summary on globalization focused on measures "to improve governance and institutions that deal effectively with the corruption problem" (15). These political problems lie at the center of development constraints; cf., among others, Kurer 1996 and Sahn 1994.

preneurial dynamics. May we be witnessing the "arrival of the post-developmental era" as hinted by McMichael (1996, 45)? Will Sachs's provocative proclamation of 1992 (3) be confirmed by a changing world system, that is, that "The scrapyard of history now awaits the category 'Third World'[26] to be dumped"?

1.2   Salient Features of Development Aid: A Practitioner's Introduction

1.2.1   Dimension

The Donor Perspective

The composition of aid by source of funding is heavily dominated by Organization for Economic Cooperation and Development (OECD) country contributions, costing the taxpayers of these countries 2–5% of their disposable income, that is, up to the value of U.S.$50 per month for a middle-income household in countries conforming to the UN's normative contribution of 1% of gross national product (GNP).[27] The target average contribution of OECD member countries, however, is 0.7%, and target achievement has consistently fallen short, rarely exceeding 0.35% on average over the past three decades.

In fact, since the early 1990s, ODA in constant-value terms has dropped steadily, reflecting a "major paradox" faced by the "international aid regime": a concerted, widely proclaimed agreement that "aid matters" accompanied by conspicuously diminishing donor generosity. "Tension between the rhetoric and the reality of aid is not a new phenomenon. But [it] has never been as pronounced as it is today" (Thérien and Lloyd 2000, 21). And a political analyst characterizes public support for aid as "a mile wide and an inch deep" (Smillie 1998, 5). Particularly threatened by a reduction in aid flows is the NGO sector, which is dominated by tax-based funding "premised on the old aid paradigm of resource transfer" and may "require both rapid and significant downsizing and a fast learning curve" (Malhotra 2000, 667). For the NGO sector this may mean a priority shift toward intensive cultivation of its private sponsor base.

For bilateral ODA the composition of shrinking funds may further tilt toward strategically motivated aid. The importance of the latter has recently been analyzed. It was found that most of all the three biggest donors, that is, the United States, Japan, and France, together accounting for nearly 60% of

---

26. Denoted by Bauer (1981, 87) as "an association of countries dedicated to the moral blackmail of a guilt-afflicted West" (frequently quoted for argumentation, e.g., Toye 1987, 5–6, and Smith 1996, 30). For an analysis of the problematic of hitherto customary country classification under superficially established "development" criteria, cf. Wolff 1995b, 24–30.

27. Achieved occasionally only by some of the smaller northern European countries, e.g., the Netherlands, Denmark, and Norway.

Table 1   Total Resource Transfers

OECD countries' official development assistance (ODA)	$51 billion
OECD countries' other official financial flows (including bilateral export credits)	30 billion
OECD countries' official grants and subsidies to NGOs, estimated	6 billion
OECD countries' private grants, mainly via NGOs, estimated	9 billion
OECD countries' total ostensive development assistance, estimated	$96 billion
Other private financial flows from OECD countries (direct investment, bank lending, etc.)	150 billion
Non-OECD countries'[a] official and private development assistance and financial flows, estimated	4 billion
Total technical and financial resource flows, estimated	$250 billion[b]

Source: OECD Development Report 2000, Statistical Annex, and author's estimates.
[a]Non-OECD members of the Organization of Petroleum Exporting Countries (OPEC), India, China, Korea, eastern European countries, and other minor, irregular sources.
[b]Equivalent to the GNP of Sweden, Switzerland, or Argentina.

total aid, prioritize strategic objectives over humanitarian and developmental objectives. For the United States this means concentration on the Near East, especially Israel and Egypt; for France, maintenance and reinforcement of economic, political, and cultural ties with its former colonies; and for Japan, rewards to supporters of its interests at UN and other international negotiations (Alesina and Dollar 2000, 55).[28] Next important criteria, by order of weight, were support of democratization, adoption of sound macroeconomic policies, and other "good governance" characteristics. Private financial flows, on the other hand, have been found to correlate most positively with "openness" to trade and investment, political and legal stability, and per capita income.

Table 1 presents a rough breakdown of total resource transfers on the basis of available information and estimates for 1999.

The Receiver Perspective

Total "ostensive" development assistance, that is, approximately 40% of the estimated total resource transfer, equals less than 1.4% of total Third World GNP. This relatively low proportion, however, grows dramatically when measured in relation to Third World government revenues or export earnings, highlighting the critical importance of these transfers for public budgets and balance of payments. In least-developed countries (LDCs) this support reached

---

28. The "friend" category in fact was found of importance in all donor decisions.

Table 2   Foreign Aid to India and Tanzania

	1980 Foreign Aid	
	India	Tanzania
Percentage of GDP	1.6	18.1
Percentage of tax revenues	16.8	106.8
Percentage of export earnings	31.2	152.8

Source: Bauer 1991.

counterproductive proportions long ago.[29] P. T. Bauer's 1991 examples (table 2), though dating back to the beginning of the third Development Decade, remain exemplary for today's dilemma.

It lies in the nature of official transfers that their impact directly benefits the monetary economy, fueling primarily the expansion of the public sector and urban consumption. This is not in the best interest of many of these societies, whose urban and public-sector consumption already outweighs their productive (predominantly agrarian, i.e., rural-based) capacity.[30] The inverse relationship between aid receipts and economic growth in a number of LDCs suggests the growth of a "rentier" mentality within a state class, which, in the interest of personal gains derived from the aid inflow, favors the perpetuation and increase of these.[31]

With regard to the impact of aid, we can differentiate between gross aid transfer and effective aid (that which reaches the target group). But to determine the "effects" of the latter, it will be necessary to distinguish between productive, unproductive, and counterproductive effects in order to arrive at what might be called net productive aid. This is normally a small fraction of the "gross aid transfer," especially under interventionist development concepts of the past.[32]

---

29. The popular argument of the mutually causal relationship between poverty and stagnation, "central theme of development economics from the 1940s to the 1970s," is contested by Bauer (1993, 9, 11): "Poverty is instanced as ground for aid; aid creates dependence and thus keeps people in poverty." Compare also Naudet (2000, 222) regarding the poverty paradigm.

30. With reference to Africa, Please (1992, 290) comments: "It is understandable that donors should see their role as addressing 'gaps' in national development programmes. However, because in most African countries the size of their financial involvement and the weight of their influence on policies and programmes are so large, what is intended to improve the 'balance' in development strategies typically seems to result in creating its own 'imbalance.' "

31. Cf. Hanisch (1993), who does not exclude promoters and managers of Third World NGOs from sharing this mentality.

32. Pessimistically assessed by Hilhorst and Sideri (1995, 41): "As for the recipient countries, many no longer need foreign aid while others have lost faith in its contribution to their development process. Those that really needed it, the smaller, poorer and more dependent, either are not receiving much or most of what they receive does not reach down to the designated target groups or activities. As a result the interest for development assistance has gradually concentrated in the

The comparatively most productive use of aid is made by receiver countries whose governments are demonstrating "good governance," that is, suppression of corruption, fiscal discipline, sound macroeconomic policies, and abidance by the rule of law. This is being confirmed by recent analysis (Dollar and Easterly 1999). The conclusion is that "societies themselves must take the lead in putting growth-enhancing policies into place" (23). Consequently, those countries qualifying for "good governance" recognition could be given the option to receive lump-sum bilateral ODA for utilization according to their considered current priorities, instead of targeted aid whose final destination often remains nebulous anyway.[33]

1.2.2   Structure

About one-quarter of ODA is in the form of grants, the balance as soft ("concessional") credit. Half of all ODA is bilateral, including most grant aid and most public funding support to NGOs.[34] The other half is given via multilateral institutions, with large shares passing through the World Bank,[35] regional development banks, United Nations Development Program (UNDP), and WFP. Over the past two decades, "agriculture and rural development" received between 12 and 20% of total ODA disbursements.

The UN specialized agencies, such as FAO, UNESCO, and the International Labor Office (ILO), are autonomous juridical entities. Their mandates are coordinated with the goals of the UN. Regular consultation with the UN Secretariat, specifically its Economic and Social Council (ECOSOC), is geared toward harmonization of individual political, environmental, and socio-economic policies. They are not subordinate to the UN Secretariat, however, but to the controlling organs constituted by the sum of their member states, their so-called governing bodies. These are structured either according to the UN equality principle (one country, one vote) or according to the weight of members' financial contribution (membership fee, share in loan fund, etc.). In FAO, a technical agency, control lies in the hands of the agency's 186 member governments, each of which has an equal vote at the biannual FAO conference. In the International Fund for Agricultural Development (IFAD), a development-financing agency, control is exercised not by the governing council of the agency's 145 member states, but by the executive board consisting of

---

vocal aid lobbies entrenched in the donor countries and in the elites of the recipient countries appropriating most of it."

33. Devaradjan et al. (1999) provides an interesting analysis of "aid fungibility," which in the extreme may benefit the "war lords," as has been revealed by recent conflict research (spearheaded by Jean and Rufin 1996, and policy-integrated by Collier 2000).

34. This "rapidly expanding worldwide network of non-state actors" has "become the most important constituency for the activities of development aid agencies" (Lancaster 1999, 288).

35. The World Bank's lending capacity, however, depends heavily on replenishments from international financial markets.

18 members with equal voting rights, representing with six votes each the interests of OECD, OPEC, and Group of 77 member countries.

The relative underrepresentation of the donor countries in the voting constituency of the multilateral technical agencies has led to a problematic division in these agencies' budget structure. A trust-fund budget, funded by individual donor contributions, has gradually come to predominate over the constitutional regular budget funded by GNP-related membership fees. Via the trust-fund facility, donor countries try to compensate for their lack of voting power by exercising direct control over "extrabudgetary" programs (e.g., many of FAO's special action programs) or individual projects that conform with individual donor-country priorities.

1.2.3   Management

In the past, aid flow has been supply-driven,[36] and this will probably continue in spite of the relative decline discussed above, as long as development aid is taken for granted by the OECD taxpayer. Fund-channeling pressure characteristically dominates the aid management, with serious consequences, such as low productivity of aid flows; excessive aid intervention in receiving countries by a growing number of competing, mostly uncoordinated, agency activities;[37] and loss of local government control over these activities ("balkanization").

Neither aid management, whose power tends to grow with increasing aid flows, nor Third World governments, for which even superfluous aid programs have advantages, such as budgetary and short-term balance-of-payment support, jobs for university graduates, and prospects for placements of nationals in an expanding international aid administration, have a serious interest in leading the shift from quantity to quality. But the change may be triggered if taxpayers in OECD countries learn of the often wasteful and counterproductive use of their contributions.

Aid funds generally pass through three major levels after being released by donors: agency policy and program coordination, agency project formulation and control, and agency project implementation. There is a tendency to window-dress agency policy to align it with donor priorities, which tend to be

---

36. This does not mean that no receiver governments have an appetite for more, especially as far as untied money or tradables are concerned. But realizable program and project concepts, as well as the institutional local infrastructure and the appropriate expertise required for their implementation, are still in short supply, a fact generally deplored by the aid-channeling community (cf. Jaycox 1994, quoted in section 3.3.2).

37. Billetoft and Malmdorf (1992) describe some of the excesses. "Presently, Bangladesh receives aid of a magnitude it is unable to absorb" (12). Quoting a Bangladeshi (Atiur Rahman): "Bangladesh could have become self-sufficient in food at least 10 years ago had there been no food aid" (19). About the NGOs' role: from the foreign donations received (partly without the local government's permission) "some 60% are apparently spent on administrative activities while merely 40% are spent directly on development purposes" (23–24).

dominated by politically effective platitudes.[38] Agency project and program formulation and control accounts for most of the agency headquarters' work. Though formally receiving policy direction from above, agency staff at this level succeeds to some degree in incorporating its considered adaptations and emphases on the basis of field-program experience, professional information, and personal and team preferences of often paradigmatic nature.[39] At the implementation level, projects enter the arena of the diverging interests[40] of participating or interfering actors (target population, government institutions, NGOs, traditional or religious authorities, local and foreign business interests, competing and overlapping activities or policies of other aid agencies), apart from the paradigmatic conditioning of the individual team members and their counterparts.

There is a constant struggle within and among these three levels. Downward pressure seeks to direct the aid flow into projects whose objectives satisfy donor expectations and the declared priorities of the UN and the respective executive agency. Upward pressure questions these priorities and the modes of their application, and seeks to integrate group and individual priorities into the formulation and conceptualization processes. Because the hierarchic structure demands caution and diplomacy ("don't rock the boat") in the upward struggle, however, policy influence in the upward direction through normal bureaucratic procedures is slow and often blocked. Instead, policy changes come about mostly from outside, for example, through publications by well-known development economists/social scientists, especially if commissioned by a powerful agency (e.g., the World Bank, UNDP, OECD, or United States Agency for International Development [USAID]) or donor consortium (e.g., Club du Sahel or the Nordic Group).

Once new ideas are articulated in influential circles or institutions, a new paradigm may start to replace the old. The whole process can, however, take anywhere from 5 to 20 years. Vested interests throughout the development hierarchy will defend the old paradigm: scientists, due to academic inertia and/or jealousy;[41] ministers of cooperation who base election campaigns and aid budgets on it; agency (and NGO) heads whose fund-channeling programs are geared to it, with vast numbers of projects in the implementation, pipeline, and identification stages, and who have molded the agency's (or NGO's)

---

38. Nett (1994, 249), referring to NGO policy: "As a rule, the task of lobbying for public funds is the responsibility of trained, politically tuned senior staff members with a thorough command of fashionable development concepts and buzzwords current at international conferences."

39. To a certain extent the planner's art of blending new instructions with old routines and preferences (see section 3.3.3 for discussion) is developed here.

40. Cf. Bierschenk and Elwert 1991, 19–21; Long and van der Ploeg 1989, 226–28.

41. Cf. Kuhn 1962, 24; Barber 1961, 596–602; for the reservations of epistemic communities to the "structural adjustment" policies introduced around the mid-1980s by World Bank/IMF economists, cf. Reusse 1993, 467, and 2001b, 23.

image to identify with it; and development workers at all levels, either because they would have to change their securely established preconceptions or, if in policy-influencing posts, because they are jealous that a new initiative outside their control may threaten their prestige.

Black (1999, 11) provides a fitting comment: "[Regarding] the very important questions as to whether donors', planners', and implementers' goals are in harmony and whether any of those goals are likely to be reflected in outcomes . . . we would do well to position ourselves at the intersection between the real world and the official world and to ask how we might cut down the number of wrecks at that intersection."

1.2.4   UN Reform

UN reform has been a topic on the international agenda over more than two decades. Pressure, especially from the U.S. government, has been increasing, and the secretary general has been put under a strict obligation to effect reforms that will produce substantial and expedient budget cuts. Analogous processes are taking place in most UN agencies.[42] Regarding chronic systemic weaknesses in such attempts, however, Rothstein's suspicion (1979, 20) that "the situation may get worse simply because living with an increasingly ceremonial process is much easier than trying to reform it" may well continue to apply, as the result of half-hearted reform is that "problems get worse, time is lost, and resources are expended."

Gallarotti (1991, 201) refers to the "critics of IO-orchestrated development schemes [which] argue that public funds of IOs [international organizations] are inferior substitutes for private investments in the Third World and tend to generate negative externalities." And Wolff (1997, 302) concludes: "Il est bien possible que le problème dépasse de beaucoup l'organisation et les méthodes du système des Nations Unies et que c'est l'ensemble du système économique international et de la prise de décision en matière de politique du développement qu'il faut réformer."

The events of 11 September 2001 have abruptly put the UN at the center of expectations for a peaceful world order. The organization may have to rigorously concentrate its resources on its political mandate in order to live up to these expectations. The Third World focus, developed disproportionately partly in response to involuntary restrictions on the organization's political potential over the past half century, will now be increasingly overshadowed by the global focus. To secure serious integration of the powerful nations into the UN system, however, rethinking on the issue of weighted votes may become imperative. (See also note 12 on page 112.)

---

42. Equally applying to bilateral aid systems, as expressed by EEC Commissioner Nielsen regarding the EU aid system: "Reform is a question of do-or-die for external aid" ("Evaluation of the EU-NGO Cofinancing Programme," synthesis report, October 2000, EEC Economic Commission [Program B7-6000], Brussels, 12).

1.3   Study Approach

1.3.1   Hypothesis

Why have the huge aid flows over four "development decades" had so little productive effect? Why is there growing doubt about the usefulness of development aid in all strata of the population, whether professionals, civil servants, taxpayers, or target-group members?

The aid world is an arena where donors, receivers, and countless middlemen meet, brought together by the magnetic stream of aid resources. This stream is fueled by fashionable development goals and concepts. Hence, once inertia takes hold, it tends to perpetuate these goals and concepts as well as to provoke new ones. The whole process has a tendency to become a powerful, self-referential perpetuum mobile.

Accompanied by a widely argued, diffuse understanding of "underdevelopment," optimistic "development" concepts are often based on superficially researched situations, problems, and needs. Nevertheless, these concepts tend to claim paradigmatic importance, that is, to serve elementary functions in the construction of development strategies. Because their creation is typically influenced by a desire to generate "needs for rectifying assistance," I refer to them as interventionist paradigms (see section 1.1.3).

The hypothesis of this study is that interventionist paradigms in Western conceptions of Third World problems lie at the root of many, if not most, ineffective aid policies. Programs and projects based on biased conceptions face implementation dilemmas, and in the attempt to negate failure they tend to attract many other typical weaknesses in aid-program management. The whole process is facilitated by ease of access to aid flows. The interventionist paradigm thus plays a central role in any analysis of behavioral patterns and pathological traits in the development-assistance arena.

I shall use two case studies from postharvest interventions in small-farmer economies, describing tenacious adherence to unrealistic paradigms and concomitant aid flows over a period of two decades, to test the validity of the hypothesis.

1.3.2   Research Methodology

As this research focused almost completely on past processes, I followed an interpretative historical methodology, selectively using (1) the relevant social, economic, and agronomic literature; (2) UN and aid-agency documentation; (3) project and evaluation reports; (4) personal communication with Third World government and aid-agency staff, experts, researchers, and local actors involved in the interventions in question; (5) extensive personal experience and observations over three decades of working for and with technical-

assistance and development-financing agencies[43] in field research;[44] analytical
and advisory technical assistance; project identification, preparation, and implementation; policy formulation and adaptation; program review and evaluation; symposia, workshops, and expert consultations; and field-project, regional office, and headquarters functions.

1.3.3   The Case Studies

The cases were selected on the basis of the following criteria: (1) policy relevance—their actual or potential role in ongoing policy debate; (2) research
relevance—their comparatively low profile in past socioeconomic research
programs and, hence, low level of transparency; (3) access to research material—their comparative accessibility due to my background knowledge and
professional contact with principal actors; (4) historical timeliness—their
relatively rounded history, covering about a 20-year paradigm life span, with
mounting symptoms of redundancy.

Two cases fulfilled these criteria particularly well: the UN-proclaimed "war
on waste," actively implemented via, for example, the FAO's Special Action
Program for the Prevention of Food Losses (PFL, 1976–99), which was principally concerned with allegedly wasteful postharvest operations in Third
World small-farmer economies; and the "cereal banks" model (a precooperative form of collective grain storage and marketing at village level), introduced
by NGOs in Burkina Faso (then Upper Volta) in the mid-1970s, which soon
assumed ideological characteristics in its heavily NGO- (donor-) promoted, bi-
and multilaterally funded expansion throughout the Sahel region.

In both cases a development program (campaign, model, ideology) evolved
on the basis of a superficially conceived but easily marketable paradigm, that
is, a construct of a Third World peasant unable to store his crop without dramatic losses and indebted to unscrupulous merchants. Hence, the latter get
their hands on the crop at a fraction of its subsequent market price, at which
the peasant is often forced to replenish stocks for his own consumption before
his new harvest. Field research, economic logic, anthropological insight, and
project failure rate has slowly but steadily disproved the paradigm in both
cases. In both cases, vested interests, inertia, and fund-channel pressure have
prolonged the life span of the paradigm far beyond a reasonable learning period. In the "war on waste," the principal promoters were crop-protection
scientists and storage engineers serving national and multinational research
and development organizations; in the "cereal banks" case, they were "grass-

43. FAO, UNDP, United Nations Conference on Trade and Development (UNCTAD), German Agency for Technical Cooperation (GTZ), World Bank, and African Development Bank
(ADB).

44. In more than 30 countries, half of them in Africa. Of particular relevance to the case stud-
ies are Belize 1964–65; Ghana 1965–68; Nigeria 1972 and 1975; Benin 1973; Togo 1973;
Cameroon 1974; Gambia 1976; Ethiopia 1977; Philippines 1978; Somalia 1980; Thailand 1981;
Bhutan 1983; Zimbabwe 1985; Egypt 1988; Jamaica 1993; Ghana 1981, 1984, 1991, and 1998.

roots," "people's participation," "cooperative marketing" idealists. Although serving the ambitions of different professional clans, both programs were rooted in the same paradigmatic conception of Third World rural backwardness and in their argumentation tended to reinforce and complement each other.

The cases have been selected from the relatively underresearched, though much politicized, postharvest sector in small-farmer economies that predominate in the Third World. Their problems are not uncommon in many other fashionable development programs in the rural/agricultural sector.

In view of the originality of much of the research material, the lack of comprehensive historical accounts of the case studies, and the potential to analyze the symptomatic weaknesses of externally induced development activities revealed by the cases, I use a broad chronological structure to describe them. By illuminating the persistence of a paradigm, the cases are demonstrations of typical, if not chronic, defects in the aid system.[45] An abstract precedes each case to orient the reader.

Chapter 3, "Analysis and Discussion," relates the cases to the broad behavioral and "pathological" spectrum of the "development business." Chapter 4, "Conclusions and Recommendations," transforms the general and case-related insights into suggestions for remedies at the macropolicy level.

The empirical path tracing the effects of a powerful paradigm is intended to unravel the Eurocentricity of many development interventions and the inefficiencies concealed by their distorted focus. Perhaps this will encourage more thorough assessment of local situations and the separation of the needs felt by the population from those superimposed by the ambitions of experts. Above all, the objective is to put long-term cost/benefit, that is, sustainability, criteria at the center of technological as well as socioeconomic feasibility considerations in screening proposals for intervention.

---

45. I may be asked whether these cases, both from the rural-agricultural environment and with geographical concentration in Africa, are sufficiently representative of the "ills" of aid to be used as a basis for general conclusions. The answer is that cohesive case study material over a complete program period is very hard to find in the field of development assistance. Rather than compiling fragmentary and often secondhand episodes from varied environments, I gave preference to these authentic cases. The conclusions drawn and final recommendations derived, however, mirror the whole of my richly composed geographical and professional experience.

Chapter 2

The Cases

2.1 The "War on Waste"

> Technology is like genetic material—it is encoded with the characteristics of the society which developed it, and it tries to reproduce that society.
>
> B. Wambi

2.1.1 Abstract

Frustrated by the disappointing results of modern production technology in Third World small-farmer economies and alarmed by the food gap of the drought years in the Sahel in the early 1970s, news of high crop-storage losses in these economies fell on fertile ground in the international development debate. Though this news was later unmasked as unrepresentative dramatization, the aid flow, triggered by well-marketed "food-loss prevention" programs, developed its own momentum and, with the help of bureaucrats and technicians with an interest in the programs' continuation, provided technical assistance against the alleged food waste for nearly two decades. The appropriation of the aid machinery was facilitated by the prevalence of the cooperative ideology paradigm of individually weak farmers in want of appropriate storage technology and exploited by merchants.

While the conceptual failure gradually emerged, the program continued largely because of professional pride, bureaucratic inertia, individual and institutional ambition, image protection, and survival motivations,[1] in the process clearly revealing some of the symptomatic weaknesses of aid program management. Those weaknesses and the persistence of the paradigm appear to be mutually supportive.

Field research has corrected the alarming assumptions of the early 1970s of postharvest food-grain losses in Third World countries of about 15–40% down to about 3–12% (5% is the most frequently reported average).[2] Today it is recognized that the allegedly weak and exploited small farmer holds more than

---

1. "The learning is that vested interests and professional predispositions can sustain an entrenched belief long after it has been repeatedly exposed as false" (Chambers 1997, 21).

2. Cf. inter alia Tyler and Boxall 1984, 7–8; Greeley 1990, 10; Compton et al. 1993, 285; and Fleischer, Waibel, and Dirksmeyer 1995, 1, 7, 8.

75% of the economy's domestic food-grain reserves.[3] These adjustments throw doubt on other powerful interventionist paradigms in the development-policy and -assistance debate.

The following is a brief chronological summary of the major events:

History. Dramatized laboratory experiments (late 1960s); Kissinger speech at World Food Conference 1974; PFL launched in 1976 with Netherlands Trust Fund support.

Development. Summary promotion of optimistic project concepts; about 200 projects up to 1992, many as follow-up, most with mixed funding from multi- and bilateral (trust fund) sources; late realization of relative irrelevance; dwindling donor support; turning to postharvest systems approach.

Results. Tying of expert and administrative resources to low-productivity program over nearly two decades; neglect of essential analytical, unbiased approach to postharvest systems.

Role of "evaluations." Limited to generally conciliatory tripartite and auto-"evaluation" exercises; occasional suppression of critical consultant inputs; no external evaluation.

Role of external criticism. "Milestone" study commissioned by World Bank (Greeley 1990) reluctantly acknowledged by executive staff; main point: reducible losses (under cost/benefit criteria) hardly exist in traditional postharvest activities.

Management response. Slow adjustment under mounting criticism, decisive response only after donor interest faded; evaluation by in-house Evaluation Unit repeatedly postponed; lack of socioeconomic expertise within the responsible management hierarchy (dominated by engineers and technologists), most pronounced during first decade of program; funding autonomy not conducive to efficiency monitoring; notorious lack of "ex post" project evaluations; PFL special action program (SAP) closed in stages over the period 1993–99.

Donor response. "Tripartite" monitoring and evaluation missions weakly manned by trust-fund donor; tendency toward mutual face-saving; phlegmatic resilience of established donor priorities; funding flows started drying up in the early 1990s.

2.1.2 History

Background

In the first two development decades, early enthusiasm for agricultural development saw much promise in economies of scale. Large collective farming and

---

3. This proportion was revealed in an OECD report on China (1995); similar results had been obtained in a survey of West African maize farm storage and marketing, covering several seasons (Reusse et al. 1968; Reusse 1976).

ranching ventures organized as state farms or cooperatives were promoted, but their general failure cast the first doubts on the applicability of economies of scale under Third World conditions.

Although the small farmer's efficiency as a producer was now reluctantly acknowledged, his role as manager of on-farm postharvest operations and primary marketing strategy was not. Outsiders were still biased against management and marketing by small-scale operators. Marketing boards and cooperatives were conceived as solutions, and "modern" technical innovations were promoted with national and donor support, facilitated by import-license and exchange-rate privileges.

Most senior government staff, especially in Africa, had graduated in Europe or North America and returned with a "modernization" bias, ready to dismiss traditional methods. Western experts, eager to instigate "change" and earn personal recognition, met with little open resistance.

Alarm Signals

In this situation in the mid-1960s, crop-storage and pest-control scientists alerted the scientific and agro-industrial community to allegedly dramatic deterioration in grain stocks in rural storage in developing countries. The observations, however, were highly localized and widely linked to simulation trials. Loss assessments were based on samples drawn from farm-held end-of-season stock in humid climates, when at least 90% of the previous harvest had been consumed and the new crop was about to be harvested, or on simulated barn-storage experiments at research stations lacking important elements of farmers' traditional conservation and management practices.[4]

Results that reported spectacular deterioration levels of 20–60% met with ready attention in postharvest industry and development-assistance circles and were quickly recognized for their fund-raising potential. To secure funds for a project, an activity, or general departmental budget support,[5] it became common practice to exaggerate loss assessments,[6] for example, by generalizing those of hybrid varieties (which accounted for a very small, mostly commercial share of cereal cultivation outside of research stations). That farmers applying traditional methods to locally adapted varieties did far better remained

---

4. See, e.g., early experiments carried out by the Food Research Institute in cooperation with the Ministry of Agriculture's Pest Control Unit at Pokuase (Ghana) in 1965–66.

5. Personal communication, NRI Crop Technology Dept., 1993. "Losses can be made to occur— . . . the more dramatic the manner in which [they are] presented, the more likely [they] are to be accepted" (Tyler and Boxall 1984, 4).

6. "Figures were bandied around carelessly . . . [N]o definition of loss [was] provided . . . [Estimates were] often meaningless[,] . . . according to one calculation [accumulating to] a grand total [pre- and post-harvest loss] of 105% . . . The highest food loss estimates [were] published in journals supported by companies selling . . . equipment. Examples are not uncommon of inappropriate technological choices being foisted upon national governments by international aid agencies in league with international companies . . . there are vested interests in high food loss estimates" (Greeley 1982, 51–52).

unknown or was conveniently disbelieved in the Western crop-storage scientific community.[7] It took time to find out why farmers behaved apparently irrationally, for example by mixing sand or ashes into their stored grain, using many thin poles to support their storage structures (to spare trees), and keeping these light (no mud-walling).[8] Some field research that deflated the assumptions of high losses in farm storage was documented as early as 1968 (e.g., Reusse et al. 1968), but did not attract the attention of policymakers in a climate of dramatization.

United Nations Initiative

Given the lively international attention paid to the alleged phenomenal food losses in developing countries, in 1968/69 the FAO's director general (Addeke Bourma) included the "war on waste" among the organization's five "selected priority areas of special concentration."[9] He extended the meaning of "waste" to include waste of land, water, and energy resources, an interpretation that entered into the World Food Conference Resolutions (November 1974).[10] Political interest focused on the food-loss phenomenon, however, especially that assumed to exist at the rural postharvest level and particularly in on-farm storage. Speeches during preparatory and main sessions of the conference abounded with references to these losses and their grave repercussions on food availability in those environments plagued by poverty and malnutrition. The following quotes from addresses of conference participants convey the tone:

[C]ar n'oublions pas qu'il est admis, actuellement, que 20% de la production mondiale des céréales des pays en voie de développement servent a nourrir des déprédateurs au cours du stockage, de breve durée, d'ailleurs.[11]

Merely stopping unnecessary waste in harvesting and storage and losses to insects and other pests would bring the world a large amount of time as we seek to increase production.[12]

---

7. "High farm losses were attractive because they blamed the farmer and invited a technological fix" (Chambers 1997, 21).

8. Personal communication from the NRI Crop Technology Dept., 1993.

9. Director general's forewords to SOFA 1968 and 1969. The other four areas were "high-yielding varieties," reducing the "protein gap," "mobilization of human resources," and "earning and saving of foreign exchange."

10. Report of the World Food Conference, UN, New York, 1975, 5.

11. Adrien Senghor, Senegalese minister of rural development, World Food Conference Proceedings, Rome, November 1974. French quotations in the case studies are included in the interest of clarity and authenticity of the argumentation. Generally, their meaning is summarized in, or self-evident from, the accompanying English text.

12. Earl Butz, U.S. secretary of agriculture, ibid.

Current losses during food storage, processing and handling could well have fed hundred millions of people . . . In Africa almost 30% of all crops . . . are lost in storage.[13]

It is estimated that, of the food actually available to individual families at the village level, 20% is lost between harvests to rodents and other pests—for lack of suitable storage. And yet, efficient storage facilities could be constructed easily, at very modest cost.[14]

The conference's optimism, that is, its confidence in the ability of international development assistance to overcome the alleged food-waste problem in developing countries, regarded as a major obstacle on the way to universal food security, was crowned by Henry Kissinger's proposal: "today we must proclaim a bold objective—that within a decade no child will go to bed hungry, that no family will fear for its next day's bread."

A more concrete target was set by the UN General Assembly (1975), following its articulation by the newly founded World Food Council, with the demand for an "at least 50% reduction" of postharvest losses in developing countries "by 1985":[15] a clear signal for FAO and other technical agencies to become involved.

Launching the Program

While the departing FAO director general, Addeke Bourma, appeared to have become more cautious about the underlying assumption of farmers' inability to avoid waste—his statement at the World Food Conference was conspicuously void of reference to this theme—the newly elected director general, Edouard Saouma, made the reduction of "crop losses . . . particularly post-harvest . . . often totaling up to 40% or more . . . to tolerable limits" one of his two primary concerns (the other being "investment leading to increased agricultural production").[16]

Consequently, the action program for the prevention of food losses (PFL) was launched as one of FAO's special action programs (SAPs) at the 1977 biannual conference, inviting member countries to pledge a minimum target of $20 million[17] as an "initiative to reduce the enormous avoidable losses of food that occur both before and after the harvest."[18]

---

13. Mustafa Tolba, deputy executive director, United Nations Environmental Program, ibid.

14. Henry Labouisse, executive director, United Nations Children Fund, ibid. Compare this with the tenor of a 1997 FAO/UN "Food Summit" feature, stressing the "need to restore indigenous knowledge on food storage and inter-cropping . . . that were once dismissed as primitive but which are now understood to protect the environment" (Okello 1996)!

15. Resolution no. 3 of the Ad-Hoc Committee of the 7th Special Session of the General Assembly, Bi-Annual Conference Report, FAO, Rome, September 1975.

16. Director general's foreword, SOFA 1976, 2.

17. Director general's foreword, SOFA 1977, 3.

18. Director general's foreword, SOFA 1978, 2.

The 1977 conference document introducing the PFL program showed the influence of the storage-engineering group of the agricultural services division, whose senior officer, a Dutch national, had been appointed PFL program coordinator—a change from the previous leadership of the crop-protection group of the plant production division, and probably not entirely unrelated to the major program pledge of the Dutch government. As a result, the interpretation of PFL shifted from "prevention of food losses" (which potentially included preharvest losses) to "reducing post-harvest losses of staple foods."[19]

The engineering/postharvest technology approach showed in the self-confidence of the program design, aiming for "straightforward and rapid" project preparations, main project activities "to be completed in 1½ years," "act[ing] as springboards for development," and "achieving a significant impact within a limited period of time" (par. 39–43). Prototype project concepts were drawn up and offered to member countries for implementation; 80% of program funds were thus earmarked for village grain stores, warehouses, and grain drying and milling equipment (par. 48).

Early Problems

On the assumption that developing countries' governments attached equal importance to food losses, they were requested to give high priority to projects in countries' food-loss-reduction programs (para. 48). Such national programs were not forthcoming, however, local administrations closer to rural reality apparently being less convinced of the claimed potential for realizable food-loss savings.

Another requirement that was not satisfactorily met was the inclusion of "loss assessments" in "all projects in order to monitor progress in loss reduction." Those assessments proved exceedingly difficult, especially as major assumptions on which the program was based were soon recognized as unverifiable.

In fact, a countercurrent developed among social scientists outside and inside the organization[20] against the modernistic self-confidence of the technicians and in favor of a much more cautious and appreciative approach to existing (local) resource-management systems. An article published in the influential FAO monthly *Bulletin of Agricultural Economics and Statistics* summarized the competitive advantages of low-cost traditional on-farm storage over other storage systems under tropical conditions, based on a comprehensive farm-storage and marketing survey in West Africa, and hinted at the errors and exaggerations in loss assessments circulating in international discussion (Reusse 1976, 2–4). Shortly afterward, painstaking survey work in south Asia and southeast Africa revealed unexpected efficiencies in traditional

---

19. Conference document C77/19 (Summary), Bi-Annual Conference Report, FAO, Rome, November 1977. The Dutch dominated in the leading responsibilities of PFL until 1989.

20. Compare, e.g., Abbott (1992, 179), chief of marketing and credit service: "The marketing group, which saw lack of incentive as a main cause of storage losses, had to keep quiet."

postharvest systems, and crop losses a small fraction of previous assumptions (Boxall et al. 1978, 124–26; TPI 1979, 1).

However, program management paid little heed to these warnings. Support, in money and in kind (pesticides and equipment), had started pouring in; project requests, so vigorously promoted, were piling up; all hands and minds were occupied with implementation.

2.1.3   Program Evolution

The "Bold" Period (1977–87)

Project requests proposed to Third World governments were drafted by ministry staff with the help of visiting headquarters staff or consultants, following basic outlines issued by the PFL unit. Project "objectives" and "justifications" drew on the following assumptions of the early interventionist decades of rural development policy:

- Small farmers were forced to sell surplus production at harvest time because, apart from indebtedness, of lack of storage capacity and inappropriate technology.
- Traditional farm-storage methods were leading to insupportably high storage losses.
- Other postproduction processes in traditional systems, that is, harvesting, threshing, drying, and primary processing at farm or rural trade level, were wasteful.
- The application of modern technology would benefit the small farmer.
- The farmer would be willing to transfer some stages in the postharvest process of his crop to facilities managed as a precooperative.

Although already contested by unbiased socioeconomic and farm-management research, these assumptions passed the project screening desk undisputed, awaiting substantiation during the projects' first (assessment) phase. Presuming substantiation as a matter of course, project inputs were committed and programmed accordingly, including the replication of technical and economic innovations on a larger scale (regional/national) in second- and third-phase project cycles.

When more and more projects revealed their inability to complete their assessment phase satisfactorily, that is, with a confirmation of the prevalence of high food losses in the existing postharvest systems, a new policy was adopted. "Detailed surveys were de-emphasized . . . to avoid situations where loss assessment becomes an end in itself rather than a means to the end of attaining project objectives . . . Rapid assessment" was now to be preferred, not aiming at absolute data but, on the basis of a general assumption of high losses, at merely "an order of magnitude"[21] indicating priority areas where "corrective measures [were] to be taken."[22] Loss "assessments" thus became meaningless, "undertaken seemingly only to justify a course of remedial action which has already been decided upon" (Tyler and Boxall 1984, 10).

This downgrading of assessment invited continued generalization and dramatization, and mitigated against the lesson learned from failures during the first years of the program, that is, that "all improved post-production methods introduced [would have to be] monitored and evaluated in qualitative and quantitative terms and compared with unimproved methods in respect of loss reduction and in the light of appropriate socio-economic criteria."[23]

The lack of serious attention given to salient criticism was particularly noticeable in regard to socioeconomic consultant inputs, as this professional capacity was hardly represented in PFL program and project management. Symptomatically, those critical inputs were often hard to trace.[24]

The repeated demand by socioeconomists for a "thorough examination of traditional practices[25] . . . at the beginning of each PFL project" ("If we do not know the exact benefits as well as the problems of traditional practices, how can we say that 'modern' practices are more economical/appropriate and for whom they may be better?") was dismissed early in the program on the grounds "that it is difficult to get this sort of information . . . that projects do not have time or money for such activities."[26]

First Reconsiderations (1982 Review and 1987 Guidelines)

In the FAO Review of Regular Program 1982–83 "[i]nadequacies of the (original) PFL Guidelines"[27] were made responsible for meager results, for example, that "the first generation projects showed vividly that sufficient provision was not made for socio-economic analysis of post-production practices to enable an adequate prior determination of the most relevant objectives,

---

21. Contrasting with the emphasis given to the need for baseline establishments by Boxall et al. (1978, 124): "because the absence of reliable and rigorously derived loss estimates has become the single most important constraint in mounting programs to improve the efficiency of post-harvest systems."

22. FAO Review of Regular Program 1982–83, Rome, 239.

23. Ibid., 252.

24. E.g., the complaint in a Review Mission (Mali) back-to-office report (John Williams/ DDC, December 1984, 1): "An important consultant report concerning socio-economic aspects of the project area was not available either in Rome or on site"; and Rosalind Eyben, socioeconomic consultant on a visit to Mali, June 1985, 2: "Unfortunately, the final version of the Funfana report [baseline socio-economic study, 1983] can no longer be traced in Rome and was never officially submitted to the Government of Mali."

25. E.g., Cynthia L. Myntti, "A Critical Assessment of the Socio-economic Implications of FAO/PFL Projects in Yemen Arab Republic, Nepal, and Pakistan," FAO, Rome, 1981, 2.

26. Minutes of AGS/PFL meeting (chaired by AGS director) on Myntti's "conclusions and recommendations" after her return from "assessment" mission, Rome, 10 December 1980, 2.

27. Obviously referring to conference document C77/19, November 1977.

activities and areas of work." It was realized that "the economic viability and social acceptability cannot be taken for granted" and that "these factors were not given adequate consideration" and (in this connection) that the "effectiveness" of training inputs "appeared to have been vitiated to a greater or lesser extent by the absence of an adequately tested and appropriate message . . . to transmit to farmers" (252).

Ten years of extensive project implementation (more than 100 projects), however, left the PFL unit with vague assumptions about the ineffectiveness of project results, as apparent from the 1987 guidelines; about the "constraints" on "widespread adoption of proven postharvest improvements" ("not easily identified"); about the lack of project follow-up by local or government initiative, deploring the frequent "examples where development projects have in effect ended in a vacuum."[28] Explanations were searched for "insufficient resources and incentives," "lack of readily and cheaply available" "inputs," too narrow scale of "exposure," and underdevelopment of governments' "awareness" of food losses and "understanding" of the postharvest system, while the crucial neglect of cost/benefit calculations and the failure of the projects to provide baseline data for such calculations were consistently overlooked.

This omission masked the projects' (and programs') reluctance to touch the basis of their raison d'être, that is, the insupportable assumption of high and readily reducible losses in local postharvest systems of developing countries.

Probably not unaware of Tyler and Boxall's excellent analysis (1984) of the comparative strength of traditional storage systems, but obviously late in giving it appropriate attention, the 1987 guidelines admitted that "early in the development of FAO's Special Action Program for PFL not enough was known about food losses in developing countries" and "not only FAO but member countries—the clients, conceived storage to be *the* problem area"; that is, "traditional farm storage, it was assumed, provided inadequate protection." More pertinently, they pointed out that "projects designed to test a technology need to do an objective job and to be able to 'fail' a technology without 'failing' as a project" (15). These were much belated insights after 10 years of the program and 40 years of the organization's existence as the world authority on information and development in food and agricultural systems.

The dilemma of the program and its projects in adapting their approach to reality is clear from project summaries presented in these guidelines. A project in Pakistan, after four years of introducing and promoting "simple storage improvement (fumigation, metal bins)" and producing impressive speculative calculations of potential wheat-loss savings if extended nationally, still "had not yet been able to test whether these methods were universally acceptable to the farming community and whether they were economic and labor saving"

---

28. R. Booth, A. Toet, L. Bevan, "Investing in Sustainable Post-harvest Programs: Guidelines for the Development of Post-harvest Efforts to Improve Food Supply: 10 Years Experience of FAO Special Action Program," FAO/AGS, December 1987, 15–26.

(17). In an Indian project, "where post-harvest losses in cereals had been estimated at 15%," "the rationale was straightforward: if village women can be
educated and motivated to adopt simple known technologies . . . food self-
sufficiency and economic self-sufficiency are easier to achieve." "Women
trainers," "front-line women workers," exhibitions, film shows, and so forth
were mobilized in a 16-month "action program" to promote "improved non-
metal storage structures and rat control measures." In the end, however, it had
to be realized that "prevention of post-harvest losses was not being given priority" in local development initiatives. The reason was sought in the "lack of
resources" (19; the more likely causes of disappointment were unrealistic
baseline and benefit assumptions).

Policy and Program Inertia

While the 1987 guidelines mixed superficiality of analysis with some valid
conclusions, the following half decade of project activities appear to have paid
little heed to the warnings and lessons contained in the document, in sporadic
observations by field staff and consultants,[29] or in occasional general policy
pronouncements.[30] The dominant impression from a random study of project
documents for the 15 program years up to 1992 is of generalities used to identify and justify projects, optimism in setting project goals, and superficiality in
impact analysis. Serious deficiencies show up, most of all in identification
and/or admission of failure; efforts to learn from past mistakes; professional
screening of project requests and proposals; and scrutiny of qualifications of
identification and preparation missions, project staff, and consultants.

Social and economic cost/benefit analysis remained grossly neglected, in
spite of excellent FAO consultant inputs such as the reports of Sandy
Stephens, V. Altarelli-Herzog, and K. A. P. Stevensen,[31] reports that deserved
to be read and discussed thoroughly by all headquarters and project staff connected with the PFL program. Neither very pertinent advice and observations
in socioeconomic consultant reports nor their persistent warnings against the
absence of socioeconomic/sociocultural expertise in PFL field missions and

29. See, e.g., Wanders (agricultural engineer) and Antony (storage entomologist): "Although
wild guesses have been made suggesting that up to 30% of food crops are lost during storage, in a
number of studies in other regions of Africa traditional storage losses have on average been
calculated in the region of 3 to 5% and it is suggested that Gambia is unlikely to be different"
("Review of P. H. Technology in The Gambia," November 1986, 11).

30. Thus, in his foreword to SOFA 1982, the FAO director general had already requested
"development policies for the future" to be "formulated on the basis of a sound understanding of
farming and husbandry systems; the human and ecological setting associated with these systems;
and the economic, political and administrative feasibility of the proposed changes."

31. S. Stephens, "A Consideration of Some Social Factors," Rome, 1980; V. Altarelli-Herzog,
"Quelles Stratégies pour une Véritable Insertion du Contexte Socio-économique dans le Program
PFL?" Rome, 1982; and K. A. P. Stevensen, "Social and Economic Aspects of PFL Activities,"
Rome, 1984.

project teams appear to have received adequate attention or follow-up by the program management.[32]

In 1990, one of the influential Economic Development Institute (EDI, World Bank) analytical case studies effectively deflated the storage-loss paradigm, giving instead due recognition to the appropriateness of locally evolved traditional methods.[33] The study concludes: "The level of storage investment that would be justified on the basis of losses alone are small, and in many cases current practices are optimal in that the cost of loss prevention are greater than the value of the losses"; and more explicitly: "Field experience suggests that even though farmers' stores are often crude in construction, the critical consideration of store hygiene, temperature, and humidity control are competently, often ingeniously, catered for" (Greeley 1990, 11). With reference to the perpetual unsubstantiated exaggerations of alleged postharvest losses in traditional systems, the study dryly summarizes: "[T]he one characteristic most commonly distinguishing high from low estimates is the time spent in the field" (ibid.).

Such "time spent in the field," that is, productive field research, tends to be a chronically neglected component in field project activities. Administrative necessities, liaison with government departments and local donor-agency representations, public relations and awareness-raising activities, elaboration of training programs and extension messages, work plans, financial and progress reports, apart from the organization of various visits by headquarters staff, tripartite agency representatives, and short-term consultants, tend to crowd out field research in development projects. Not without influence is the fact that effective fieldwork involves temporary separation from urban conveniences, social circles, and security. When the project office is also far away from the project area, lack of progress in adapting project goals and strategies to local reality is no surprise.[34]

"Receding Horizons": The Unending Project Cycles

Even before projects came to grips with reality, they were often lumbered with the preparation and promotion of satellite and/or follow-up project docu-

---

32. Armbrüster and Dresrüsse (1993, 81) refer to this neglect: "No significant evidence can presently be discovered that during the last ten years this situation has improved. No applied guidelines for socio-cultural survey and analysis of post-harvest systems exist."

33. "The myth of high average cereal losses in farm-level post-harvest systems is slowly but firmly being dispelled" (Greeley 1990, 14).

34. Similar constraint often jeopardized consultant inputs; e.g., when due to delays in coordinating an important socioeconomic mission to a PFL project in Tanzania, "effective exposure to the field was reduced to a mere 15 days, a far cry from the original 6 week schedule" (N. Spaarman et al., "Socio-economic Factors in the Farm-Level Post-harvest System," consultant report, FAO [AGS], Rome, February 1990, 1); and "Due to shortage of petrol, only one field visit was made" (Russel, PFL project review mission, Nepal, April 1989, annex, 10).

ments.[35] This situation appears to apply to many aid-supported activities. It has been classically portrayed in a PFL consultant report: "The project was designed without indicators; as a result it cannot be rigorously evaluated. It was developed to follow on after a previous project; no external evaluation was conducted before this project was designed and approved. There was no structure in place to ensure that [it] incorporated the experience that had been gained in the previous projects; there was no forum for analysis and discussion . . . Like the horizon that recedes as you walk toward it, the future of the project inputs and activities is seen as never coming. Another follow-on project will be designed, the dollars and technicians will continue."[36]

Two years later, another consultant team, evaluating a follow-up to the project portrayed above, came up against the same program weakness; the follow-up project again lacked a "formal logical framework in the project document linking objectives, outputs and project activities with indicators of impact or achievement. This had serious repercussions on assessing the impact of the project," which "will, at its termination, have completed ten years of project work in Sierra Leone without any formal assessment of what the priorities should have been in reducing post-harvest losses in the most effective and efficient way for farmers and their families."[37]

As a confirmation of this chronic inconclusiveness of a decade of PFL project inputs in Sierra Leone, as well as of the stereotypical superficiality of aid-program lobbying in general, a programming mission to the country in August 1992 reiterated that "domestic food availability could be significantly increased if the level of post-harvest losses were reduced," deploring that "lack of systematic information about the magnitude of the losses . . . and the costs of reducing them means that it is not possible at this stage to make an assessment of which problems it would be most cost-effective to tackle, and in what way," and therefore included the conventional elements of the initial PFL project design of the late 1970s, such as "detailed studies" on "the magnitude of post-harvest losses," "small-scale, low-cost processing technologies that reduce food losses and also increase household incomes," and the "creation"

35. Symptomatic is the criticism included in a consultant report reviewing a PFL project in Nepal (Boxall, "Report on Project Review Mission" [Nepal], FAO [AGS], Rome, September 1982, 2): "It should be noted that the project manager was under pressure at a very early stage to direct his attention away from project activities and to prepare a draft plan for future expansion of the Rural Save Grain Program. It would have been entirely appropriate to have done this at the end of the project and indeed this was clearly indicated in the project document. It would appear that the appointment of staff to the project was conditional upon the preparation of the document."

36. Ruth Anne Homeyer-Mitchell, Alimani Kargbo, and A. F. in t'Veld, "Improvement of Rice Milling Capacity at the Village Community Level, Sierra Leone," FAO consultant report, Freetown and Rome, May 1989, 57, 59.

37. D. J. B. Calverley, C. D. Smit, and I. Cole, "Improvement of Crop Post-harvest Practices at the Village Level, Sierra Leone," FAO consultant report, Freetown and Rome, February 1991, vii, 53.

of a "national body to be permanently responsible for collecting and analyzing data on post-harvest food losses and coordinating the activities of the various agencies."[38] Consequently, a UNDP project, formulated in February 1993, harbored most of the stereotypes of the early PFL history, including "rehabilitation and development of crop storage and processing facilities," "construction schemes for . . . drying floors and stores," "support . . . of Farmers Associations," and "promotion" of "village level food processing activities."[39]

The old excessive loss estimates remained in use, possibly perpetuated by ignorance or complacency or in order to maintain donor interest in project proposals. Thus, despite 14 years of PFL work in Tanzania and the gradual but steady realization that losses in farm storage were generally not dramatic (e.g., 2–3% of the basic staple crop, maize, according to two project reports around 1990),[40] the introduction to an "Evaluation Mission" report commissioned locally by the UNDP-funded PFL project in May 1991 starts with a stereotypical generalization: "It is estimated that 70 to 80% of the total grain production in Tanzania is retained at the farmers' homestead for prolonged periods. This leads to post-harvest losses amounting to 30% or 40% of the total crops due to poor storage management, insects, rodents, mould and pilfering."[41]

Crisis of Confidence

Although the PFL program reacted very slowly to the mounting internal and external criticism, toward the end of the 1980s a "crisis of confidence" invaded the program. As summed up by a program-review consultant,[42] the old certainties had been demolished by project experience and with them a coherent approach to the problem of the prevention of food losses. From about that time, the program lost its well-defined focus, and, consequently, so did the projects. The range of commodities increased, including harvesting and marketing components of some sort. In short, there were projects of all sorts in many countries under the PFL umbrella, so much so that they defy categorization. Yet again, however, it often turned out that the solutions proposed were not economically acceptable to the individuals involved. A policy paper for an international meeting on postharvest matters added a constructive direction to

38. UNDP/FAO Agricultural Sector Review/Programming Mission (Sierra Leone), vol. 1, "Findings and Recommendations," UNDP, Freetown, and FAO, Rome, August 1992, pp. 12.25, 12.26.

39. "Integrated Rural Development, Food Security, and Natural Resources Management Program: Terms of Reference for Collaborative Mission," UNDP, Freetown, February 1993, 8, 9.

40. Spaarman et al., "Socio-economic Factors," p. 3; "Summary of the Tripartite Project Review: Reduction of Post-harvest Losses through Storage," FAO/UNDP, Dar es Salaam, January 1990, 2. While these reports have comparatively high credibility, the establishment of scientifically accurate loss assessments in the traditional farm-storage environment is practically impossible.

41. Hauli and Kidunda, "The Role of Village Stores in the Post-harvest System," UNDP, Dar es Salaam, May 1991, 2.

42. Personal communication, FAO, November 1993.

the critique: "With the declining importance of parastatal grain storage and the growing realization that storage losses in 'traditional' systems are by no means dramatic and in fact hard to reduce cost-effectively, the search for improvement potentials drove wider into the post-harvest systems arena" (Reusse 1995, 16).

While still sailing under the food-loss-prevention banner, though with dwindling donor support,[43] internal program discussions finally considered abandoning the long-defended and long-defeated paradigm.

> With the objective to increase food availability, efforts were directed to developing interest in farm level post-harvest technology in LDC countries. This was based on four assumptions:
> - that traditional farm level post-harvest technology was the cause of substantial food losses;
> - that techniques were available or could be developed to prevent these losses;
> - that it would be profitable for farmers to adopt these new techniques;
> - that food availability for the hungry would increase once improved techniques were introduced and adopted.
>
> Recent evidence suggests that these assumptions are more often false than true. (internal reflection paper, 3–4, quoting Greeley 1990, 8)

It was now admitted that only "small quantities of loss occur at multiple points along the post-harvest chain, several of which in normal circumstances are difficult to reduce below their existing levels." Furthermore, "[i]n traditional systems, there is normally a balance between production and post-harvest practices which are mutually adequate and supporting and allow efficient functioning of the food chain" (ibid., 2).

A sociological consultancy for a PFL project in Laos pointed to the low priority of postharvest losses among farmers: "les pertes . . . ne sont pas considérées un véritable problème . . . par les paysans . . . [Ils] considèrent d'être à mesure de contrôler les pertes, s'ils le veulent . . . Pendant la réunion finale, sollicitées à maintes reprises sur l'utilité de protéger la récolte, les paysans ont montré de préférer d'autres arguments de discussion pour eux plus intéressants et importants."[44]

---

43. A PFL internal reflection paper of early 1993 ("Background and Program Design," 12) speaks of the need for "a promotion campaign to dispel possible misunderstandings on the part of some donors" and of "their lack of perception/appreciation of the current PFL strategies."

44. L. Cremona and S. Phommalyvong, "Développement d'un Système Intégré de Prévention des Pertes Après-Récolte au Niveau Villageois," UNDP/FAO, Vientiane, September 1994, 12.

The Way Out

Internal reconsideration, much influenced by Greeley's study, came late[45] and was not transformed into official statements, published positions, or new guidelines for field project staff. Instead, attention was diverted from the more obvious failure of the program to new themes for its perpetuation, such as production-to-consumption process (PCP) analysis and development. This diversion did not prevent a general loss of confidence in the program, in-house as well as outside. UNDP and trust-fund inflows as well as Regular Program support ceased. At the end of 1993, the PFL unit lost its largely independent SAP status and became temporarily subordinated to the Marketing and Credit Service. In early 1995, the unit was dissolved, its staff distributed between the four technical services (marketing, engineering, agro-industry, and farm management) of the Agricultural Services Division. For the time being, the relative importance of the postharvest sector became again untraceable in the organizational structure of FAO.

Later in the same year, at the annual Group for Assistance on Systems for Grains after Harvest (GASGA) meeting, the FAO statement admitted that "assumptions made at the beginning of the PFL program concerning . . . assessment of losses, . . . reduction of these losses, . . . [and] abandonment of traditional practices in favor of modern technologies are no longer held as valid" (FAO 1995). The principal scientific paper presented at the meeting concluded that "technological improvements that were offered in the past have seldom been adequate to the problems and were little cost-effective" and that the "strategy focusing on the technical aspects of minimising food loss in storage, handling and processing . . . has come to an end."[46] The former director of the Agricultural Support Systems Division (AGS), who had helped to dismantle the PFL dogma[47] during his short term with FAO (1992–94), opened the GTZ-hosted meeting, by proposing three "paradigm changes":[48] from the perception of a straight "technology transfer" approach to one integrating the

---

45. Already in 1983 a PFL project report had warned against the dramatization of produce losses and underestimation of traditional knowledge and skills in the prevention of crop losses. "Il faut retenir notamment que les pertes après récolte au niveau de l'exploitation sont moins spectaculaires qu'on les estime de prime abord. Le producteur, très conscient de la nécessité de préserver sa production à différents stades post récolte, s'entoure de toutes les précautions pour en perdre le moins possible" ("Projet Pilote de Réduction des Pertes Alimentaires en Milieu Rural" [Mali], FAO, Bamako and Rome, 1983, 9, "Conclusions et Recommandations du Projet").

46. G. Fleischer, H. Waibel, and W. Dirksmeyer, "Future Priorities in Post-harvest Systems Development: The Role of Donor and Development Agency Support with Special Reference to GASGA," Hannover University, June 1995, 2, 8.

47. A dogma well highlighted by Aldermann and Shively 1991, with reference to the still circulating postharvest-loss assumptions "in the neighborhood of 20–30 percent of production in developing countries": "The empirical evidence of this range is not known; the assumption is so widespread, however, that it appears to command the respect that in other cultures is reserved for the utterance of the hoary elders" (46).

48. With the full support of the former PFL coordinator representing FAO at the meeting.

"socio-cultural, political, and economic conditions" under which the technology is to be applied; from the reliance on "state and government" structures to the realization of the "consequences of implications of privatization and de-regulation"; and from a "mono- or multi-disciplinary to a systems approach." He challenged the meeting "to pick up the economic opportunities implied in the post-harvest sector by reducing transaction cost and increasing the value added" and to "integrate the sector into action plans for poverty alleviation,"[49] while making no mention of PFL in his presentation.

The "phantom war" (Reusse 1995, 37) against food waste in traditional societies was over. More politely expressed, it was "no longer claimed that improvement in post-harvest activities will . . . make a significant contribution to the total amount of food available to the consumer."[50]

With regard to a critical review of the 20-year PFL program experience, at the GASGA meeting the FAO representative announced that the organization had "started the review of the PFL projects in the three continents as well as an analysis of a sample of projects related to loss assessment"; however, "These documents will not be published" (2). On inquiry (1997), it became apparent that, partly due to lack of funds, this review project had largely remained dormant. However, supported by funds committed by a resolution of the FAO biannual conference in November 1996 for the continuation of a PFL successor unit in the organization's structure[51]—which led to the establishment of a Post-harvest Systems Management Unit within the Agro-industries Service of the AGS—a fair number of country reviews had been completed by 1999 and served as a meager basis for a synthesis consultant report.

2.1.4   Results

Nearly 250 PFL projects, at the cost of approximately U.S.$130 million in development aid, added to the proliferation of aid-program activities in developing countries, most of them LDCs, where the few government facilities tend to be overstretched and/or marginalized by aid-sponsored activities. As a result, technical-assistance personnel and qualified national counterpart staff (always a scarce commodity) were locked into projects that for the most part lacked realistic targets, unbiased field research, and impact assessment. Consequently, their productivity in terms of local development benefits and their personal gains in experience and training have generally been poor.

The concentration on the alleged problem of physical waste distracted from the need to establish a permanent comprehensive postharvest systems support

---

49. Opening address by Günter Dresrüsse (director of the subdepartment for agriculture, forestry, and emergency operations, GTZ), annual GASGA meeting, Eschborn, June 1995, 3–4.

50. D. J. B. Calverly and C. du Marchie Sarvas, "Improving the Efficiency of Food Production Systems," FAO/AGS Consultants Report, Rome, March 1995, 6.

51. Emanating from the rejection by a group of 14 member countries of a council proposal to abolish the PFL program.

facility, for example, a postharvest (including marketing) systems analysis and development division (Reusse 1995, 14) within ministries of agriculture as well as in FAO's department of agriculture.

While trial and error, superficial enthusiasm, and paradigm resilience are characteristic fringe phenomena in aided "development" activities, in this case the time it took to come to terms with reality, that is, 20 years, was much longer than necessary. Many real assistance needs in the postharvest arena, such as macroeconomic policy support for market and trade liberalization, rural transport and communication systems, and so forth, received inadequate attention over this period.

2.1.5   Role of Evaluations

Generally, there are four types of evaluation of development activities: (1) tripartite evaluation, a normal management requirement for projects funded by UN or other trust-fund sources, carried out by an "independent" team composed of consultants nominated by the funding agency (donor), the recipient government, and the executing agency; (2) in-house program/project evaluation, for example by the evaluation service of the executing agency; (3) auto-evaluation, through a program or project officer and a program- or project-contracted consultant; and (4) external evaluation by a consultant team, contracted by UN or donor consortia, uninvolved in the regular management or control of the responsible organizations or any of their programs.

Tripartite Evaluation

Tripartite evaluations have been the most common type of evaluation of PFL activities. Apart from problems of staffing and coordination, the need to arrive at consensus produces compromise. The mission reports rarely reveal project shortcomings in the decisive way needed to induce compulsory corrective action, especially if this could threaten the survival or reputation of a project.[52] The three parties represented on such a mission share historical responsibility for the project concept and performance, as they sanctioned it in the first place and exercised control (funding agency) and counterpart (national agency) functions supportive of the project management (executing agency). All three tend to safeguard vested interests in continued aid flows to the project and its future successors. Thus, saving face and not rocking the boat are unwritten principles. Breaking these can involve the risk of discredit. These reports often contain relevant criticism, however, for those willing to read between the lines. Outspoken criticism is sometimes found in the annex, but this rarely finds its way into the official summary of the report.

This constitutional limitation of the effectiveness of tripartite evaluations requires very attentive reading and interpretation by those responsible for project and program management, in order to translate the essential messages

---

52. See also p. 48 with regard to hesitancy about formal intervention.

into further inquiry, where necessary, and corrective action. The requisite attention and follow-up from program management (executing agency) and control (funding agency) were lacking in the case of PFL activities; otherwise it is difficult to explain the perpetuation of identified misconceptions through a series of evaluated projects.[53] As a long-time PFL consultant deplored: "If rigorous evaluating procedures are not established and the results of evaluators not interpreted by those qualified and competent there can be no authoritative assessment of what should be the priorities in any follow-on projects."[54]

Any reinforcement of the role of evaluation will have to address the funding constraint. Evaluation is still treated as a supplementary responsibility instead of a central one in development assistance. In FAO, for example, a mere 0.4% of the regular budget has been available for the operation of the organization's evaluation service during recent years.

In-House Program Evaluation

Only one in-house program evaluation through the evaluation service was extended to PFL—in 1982. This evaluation revealed major shortcomings of the program, such as exaggerated loss estimates, the self-confident reliance on technological solutions, the lack of time and depth given to the project identification/formulation process—especially with regard to the analysis of the prevailing food-loss situation, farmers' practices, and socioeconomic conditions—and the absence in the program of socioeconomic expertise at all levels.[55] In summary, the memo accompanying the submission of the report states: "As you can see from the review, the PFL program is not on the right track and needs adjustments, perhaps significantly, in terms of its basic approach, implementation strategy and coordination within the structure of the organization."[56]

As is not uncommon with evaluations, particularly in-house ones, the draft report was followed by defensive argumentation and ended on the shelf reserved for "confidential," "strictly restricted" working documents, its potential explosiveness defused by high-level protection of the program's prestige. It was felt that the detailed report was overly critical in that it concentrated on the negative aspects of the program and overlooked many positive achievements, and might give the uninformed reader the impression that basically everything was wrong with the PFL program.

After the strong though contested warnings of the first report, the program should have been reevaluated after three to five years at the latest. But no reevaluation has been carried out. From the late 1980s, repeated proposals

---

53. See examples given on pp. 39–40.

54. Calverley, Smit, and Cole, "Improvement of Crop Post-harvest Practices," 53.

55. "Review of the Prevention of Food Losses Program" (draft), Evaluation Service, FAO/ PBE, Rome, February 1983, 11–12.

56. Memorandum from Chief PBEE to Director PBE, Division of Program, Budget, and Evaluation, 9 February 1983.

have been made by the Division of Program, Budget, and Evaluation (PBE), yet PFL used various arguments to delay implementation, such as the wish to complete a series of autoevaluations (program-internal) of PFL country programs prior to an overall program evaluation through PBE Evaluation Service (PBEE).

An in-house PBEE evaluation combining external and tripartite evaluation criteria was extended to a small number of Italian-funded PFL projects at the request of the FAO/Italy Technical Monitoring and Review Panel.[57] This report did not analyze the viability of project objectives (the results were unavailable due to extraordinary delays in implementation of the projects) but did indicate a number of weaknesses in design and execution of these projects, including

- lack of clarity in project rationale and expected development results;
- overoptimistic scheduling, significant implementation delays, and lack of rectifying action;
- excessive lead time in procurement of project equipment;
- unclear distribution of reporting responsibilities and difficulties in obtaining timely information;
- unclear commitment (at outset) to procure only Italian equipment, causing subsequent delays, apart from the principal disadvantages (maintenance and spare parts, etc.) involved in such procurement restriction; and
- imprecise and overoptimistic stipulation of government-counterpart commitments, causing serious delays in project activities.

While these findings are not necessarily representative of the conceptual viability of PFL projects in general, they did identify areas requiring greater attention. They pinpointed the obvious time pressure on the responsible headquarters unit, which invited superficiality in project conceptualization and preparation.

Autoevaluation

Most actors in the aid business, particularly in the NGO arena, favor auto- (or self-) evaluation. It normally produces positively biased assessments with image-cultivating elements. Regarding the above-mentioned program-internal PFL project evaluations, for example, the first one, completed in Nepal, November 1992, was conducted with major participation of AGS Engineering and Farm Mechanization Service staff who had played a major role in designing and monitoring the PFL projects in Nepal. Not surprisingly, the appraisal of 1992[58] contained assumptions and omissions (e.g., the substantial subsidy

57. PBEE, "Evaluation of Italian-Funded Projects within the PFL Program," Rome, October 1987.

58. "Appraisal of PFL Activities in Nepal," Kathmandu and Rome, November 1992, 9, 10, 26, 37–38.

component involved)[59] very similar to those of a project-review mission report written three years earlier and, accordingly, presented the program as a success. Various analyses carried out by consultants had raised serious doubts about the sustainability of the principal innovation, the metal farm-household storage bin, which was promoted and subsidized through a sequence of five PFL/Nepal projects.[60]

As long as the subsidy situation remains opaque, an evaluation exercise is incomplete, if not meaningless. The example demonstrates the problematic function of autoevaluation.

External Evaluation

No external program evaluation was carried out. Although potentially the most useful, in particular if past and present impact and local sustainability is included, such evaluations are rare in multilateral development activities.

Regular reports by FAO's external auditors may contain fragmentary observations on PFL projects, but they are difficult to retrieve due to restricted access to these reports. Furthermore, while these reports "reveal problems concerning the design of the projects, backstopping by the agency and efficiency in implementation," they "are less concerned with potential impact on the target groups and do not analyse the strategy of the activities vis-à-vis the specific needs for assistance of the specific countries" (DANIDA 1989, 87).

However, a number of weaknesses that were identified by a Scandinavian team of external evaluators studying approximately 20 (not specifically PFL-related) FAO projects within "an assessment of multilateral development agency activities in four Asian and African countries" appear to have been shared at that time by several PFL projects surveyed in the present study and shall therefore be briefly quoted (DANIDA 1991, 41–48).

Project objectives are in most cases overambitious.[61]

---

59. Twenty-five to fifty percent of ex-factory or border price, plus provision of transport (FAO project reports TCP/NEP 0106, November 1982, 22; and GCPP/NEP/037/AUL, November 1989, annex 3).

60. Already in 1981, Myntti identified this innovation as inappropriate for the average Nepalese small farmer (consultant's visit to PFL/NEP/001, FAO (AGS), Rome, "Critical Assessment of the Socio-economic Implications," 17–19); Shuyler reached a similar conclusion (report of visit to Nepal, November 1980, 2); the Agricultural Projects Servicing Centre, Nepal (APROSC) consultant report ("A Study on Farm Level Grain Storage Practices in Nepal," 1982, 117), restricting the potential feasibility of the bin to one region only (Terai); a Rural Save Grain project technical paper ("Review on Storage of Food Grains and Practices," October 1986, 4, 12); and doubt expressed by the FAO/Netherlands mission regarding sustainable private-sector involvement ("Interim Report, Field Visit to Nepal," May 1988).

61. "The objectives in many of the project documents are by all standards unrealistic. It is slightly surprising that the proposals have been approved by both the recipient institutions and the funding agencies . . . [This] may be attributed to the mechanism for funding FAO's activities

Institutional design . . . [often] lack[s] a realistic assessment of the role, mandate and capability of the implementing organization.

Hardly any of the reviewed documents include a financial and economic assessment of the viability of the proposed activities.

Most field project documents lack a proper socio-economic assessment of the prevailing living conditions of the ultimate target group, i.e. usually the smallholder.

Few attempts seem to have been made to establish functional links to other donor assisted activities.

[Many problems arise due to i]nsufficient analytical work carried out prior to the preparation of the project document, and FAO's difficulties in detecting and rectifying basic design flaws during implementation.

FAO, the donors and the implementing institutions all seem to postpone the necessary formal changes in project strategies until the formulation of a new phase [follow-on project].[62]

The DANIDA report was unusually harsh in its criticism, of which FAO was only one target. Its objectivity might be open to argument. The projects included might have been unrepresentative of the responsible technical agencies' general performance. However, any attentive observer of project performance in the field will find a good many impressions confirmed; again, this is not restricted to FAO projects.

OECD Survey

As the self-confidence of the development-assistance establishment weakened from about the mid-1980s, agencies became more aware of their evaluation needs. An OECD review (1990) reflected this trend, at least for agency-internal evaluation systems. The review included all important donor and multilateral agencies, though not FAO.

An analysis of the survey report reveals three dimensions in the evaluation spectrum that were insufficiently catered for in respondents' actual or planned use of evaluation: (1) the need for (uncompromising) external evaluation; (2) the need for ex post evaluation (at the time, 1990, carried out by only 1 in 20 respondents, the Inter-American Development Bank [IDB]); and (3) the need for thematic goal (or target) evaluation. Precisely these dimensions were missing at FAO. Their inclusion would have helped programs such as PFL to be

---

[by which project partners are] forced to develop proposals, which are attractive to the donors" (DANIDA 1991, 42).

62. The DANIDA 1989 (Nepal) appraisal adds: "The reporting system is basically concerned with financial and management issues and does not address issues related to impact and effectiveness."

adapted, transformed, or curtailed much earlier, freeing resources at headquarters, field, and recipient-government levels for more productive application.

2.1.6   Role of External Policy Critique

Few publications have as yet critically dealt with the postharvest food-loss assumptions and other rural-development paradigms related to the postharvest sector. The most influential is probably the EDI (World Bank) study by Martin Greeley (1990), which followed Tyler and Boxall's less noticed TPI article (1984).

While the Tyler and Boxall article certainly influenced postharvest policies within the Natural Resources Institute (NRI, formerly TPI), an important British development institution, Greeley's study enjoyed increasing influence within the donor community and multilateral agencies. In FAO, however, both publications, especially the EDI study, seem to have remained practically unnoticed or received very low key attention. Only after the EDI study was used in an informal PFL analysis in 1993 did key professionals concerned with the program ask for copies. The initial reaction of the PFL unit was defensive, pointing at the geographic limitation of the author's experience, primarily fieldwork in Asia (mainly Bangladesh).[63]

A critical summary statement on PFL appeared in *Food Policy* in an article entitled "Quo Vadis, FAO?" "After 15 years of extensive project implementation (200 completed projects by 1992) under the paradigmatic assumption of excessive losses in small-farmer post-harvest, particularly storage systems, it has now become generally accepted that these losses are moderate due to generally efficient local resource management systems under prevailing environmental conditions and that further reduction via innovative means is hard to achieve in a cost-effective manner" (Reusse 1993, 467).[64] And in a strategy analysis for GASGA, of which FAO is a prominent member: "Since nearly all innovations promoted were thus based on wrong assumptions, it cannot surprise that so few have been implemented with lasting effect, and of those few nearly none (including 'cement drying floors' and 'metal bins') have proved yet to be sustainable without continued subsidization" (Reusse 1995, 8).

The fact that most technical and policy-directing professionals concerned with PFL programs within and outside FAO accepted these criticisms of post-

---

63. Personal communication from PFL and AGS staff, March 1993.

64. Provocatively the article continued: "Why did not FAO come out ahead of the above cited publications [referring to Greeley 1990 and Berg and Kent 1991] with a self-critical, mind-opening study on these subjects? Why is the organization (or its staff) under-represented in objective international discussion? Why does it leave the initiative to catalyse new thought to others, while it has the potential of drawing on the richest experience in the fields of its mandate? Why does it tend to be late in realizing the decline of paradigmatic or fashionable approaches such as (in the past) large-scale irrigation, settlement schemes, high-input agriculture, market and price interventionism, or (more recent) aid project proliferation and the food aid lobby?" (Reusse 1993, 468).

harvest loss-prevention programs shows that the ice of resentment against critical analysis of the PFL paradigm had been broken.[65]

2.1.7   Management and Donor Response

There is a strong relationship between agency management and donor response: new development initiatives might originate from either of the two. Laying off a program, often accompanied by a paradigm change, is rarely promoted by agency management, but is rather a result of dwindling donor interest. As long as funds keep flowing into a program, agency management is reluctant to drop it or even to change it.

Thus, without a full and objective account of the program results and lessons learned, when enough donors showed—to use agencyspeak—"their lack of perception/appreciation of the current FAO/PFL strategies,"[66] agency management support for the program declined, the program was downgraded, and its termination was decided on early in 1995 and completed in 1999.

Among the factors contributing to the decline in donor interest may have been published criticisms, as discussed above. The influence of other factors, such as bilateral and internal UNDP program and project assessments, requires more research. As pointed out in section 1.2.3, on the donor side there is inertia in favor of established areas of concentration and a related tendency by fund-channel operators to resist the consequences of internal evaluation. Published criticism is more effective because of its potential to influence the political base of donor institutions.

Personal field observations by members of donor committees or development-finance management can also have a remarkable impact, as indicated by the effect of cereal-bank visits by an influential member of the Program pour la Restructuration des Marchés Céréaliers (PRMC) donor committee, reported in case 2 (see p. 65).

2.1.8   Lessons Learned

Nothing is more important in development assistance than the objective identification of real assistance needs.

Any intervention needs to be programmed with great care, adapted to local conditions, and tested in a pilot project prior to any consideration of larger-scale replication.

Pilot projects need to be intensely monitored and their results thoroughly analyzed and publicized, or otherwise made accessible to all participants in the professional field concerned, before their use as constructive base for project design is given the green light.

---

65. E.g., FAO, then chairing GASGA, supported commissioning the strategy paper from the writer of "Quo Vadis, FAO."

66. Cf. "Background and Program Design."

Superficial field reports and project documents must be rejected; both must provoke solid analysis, discussion, and technical, operational, and/or policy-relevant action (or at least reaction) from the concerned headquarters units.

Evaluation missions must have independent status, supported by appropriate selection of mission members, clear terms of reference, and adequate funds for expansion of the mission period if necessary for satisfactory completion, and must be backed by an institutional culture "valuing systematic learning for improvement."[67]

The implementation of such quality-oriented policies requires an increase of agency cost allowance, to facilitate better execution of headquarters functions (operational and normative).

2.2   Cereal Banks

2.2.1   Abstract

The same paradigmatic concept of reality as in case 1, that is, that of the indebted peasant in want of efficient storage facilities, forced to oversell, and doubly exploited by traders,[68] lies at the base of the cereal-bank (CB) model. The difference is that here the principal promoters are collective-action protagonists (instead of storage engineers/postharvest technologists) with equal if not higher fund-raising efficiency.

---

67. Masakatsu Kato, head of FAO Evaluation Service, to the author, November 1998.

68. The paradigmatic denigrating of the trader as exploitative, cheating, and monopolizing is a relic of the early European cooperative movement, which mobilized ethnic (notably anti-Semitic) and class-struggle sentiments, in alliance with a propensity of the civil servant (national and international) to distrust and envy the merchant for his uncontrollable income, superior access to information, and mobility. "That a conflict exists between the fundamental social tendency to try to preserve old ways and these convention breakers who want to try something new helps explain why entrepreneurial activities not only are the driving force of market activities and society as a whole, but are also resented, envied, and ostracized by the society they disrupt and rejuvenate" (Choi 1993, 9). The superior economic and social efficiency of private over collectively organized trading activities in competitive markets, especially in the West African subregion where most CB programs have been promoted, is today "more or less universally acknowledged" (to quote a policy statement of the FAO unit responsible for agricultural marketing and credit policy, FAO/AGSM 1996, 2). This acknowledgment has been convincingly spearheaded and substantiated by P. T. Bauer since his fundamental analysis *West African Trade* (1963). Numerous case studies, among the earliest Reusse et al. (1968) on grain marketing, have verified his stance. "Traders and Development" (Bauer and Meier 1994) provides an excellent portrait of the indispensable role of traders in development, e.g., in "the husbanding of scarce resources, notably capital"; in "providing credit to their farmer customers, which facilitates both production for the market and capital formation on the farm"; and in becoming "pioneers of manufacturing and processing activities." Regarding the development blockage in many Third World countries during the past "development decades," it concludes: "The maltreatment of traders and the suppression of trading activity in many LDCs, especially in Africa and to some extent in South Asia, have been contributory factors to economic stagnation, retrogression, and even collapse, including reversion to subsistence production with all its hazards" (140–42).

The idea behind the CB model is to transfer primary storage and marketing of cereal crops from farm-household to village (collective-enterprise) level. The program is run as a quasi-precooperative, tutored organization that, with the help of an initial capital grant in the form of donated grain stocks and store construction, extends consumption loans in kind during the off-season and earns profit from surplus marketing.

Instead of fulfilling their promise, that is, benefiting small farmers by letting them reap the rural merchant's alleged profits and accumulating communal grain-reserve stocks, CBs have suffered trading deficits and storage losses hitherto unknown to this extent in farm storage. In addition, low repayment rates on credit sales contribute to the phenomenon of shrinking assets and operational scale. For the large majority, the only hope for survival is recognition as local agents in a decentralized public food-security reserve and distribution system, which is contestable in view of the experience of CBs' inability to keep grain in good condition for more than the brief dry-season interharvest period. Despite CB promoters' impressive defense of an outworn paradigm, its survival hinges entirely on donors' (now fading) willingness to provide the continual technical and financial support on which nearly all CBs depend.

The following is a brief summary of the major events and problems of the CB movement:

History. Promotion of CB establishment as NGO-driven activity of grassroots organizations since the mid-1970s in Burkina Faso, expanding to other Sahel countries during the 1980s; sporadic occurrence in other parts of Africa and Asia (Laos, Nepal); financed mainly through food aid and bilateral funding of NGO activity.

Development. Cumulative number of "foundations," to date probably 6,000–8,000, most of which are nonoperational or dissolved; disproportionate financial, management, and training support through numerous NGOs; growing donor frustration.

Results. Tying of resources to inappropriate activity; importing lobbyism, embezzlement, corruption, and indebtedness into rural communities; retarding private trading activities, while adding nothing to the general wealth or food security of the population.

Role of "evaluations." Autoevaluations, mainly through NGOs, tend to select "success stories," feature chronic difficulties as infant problems, claim still more support; multi- and bilateral technical assistance and food-aid programs show similar weaknesses; few attempts of theme or target evaluation inconclusive in the face of a glaring lack of performance records.

Role of external criticism. Solid USAID-commissioned report (Berg and Kent 1991) evaluates CBs as a misconceived institution; advises donors to reconsider continuation of support; demands proper financial auditing.

Agency/NGO response. To date still no truly representative survey or professional audit of CBs; thriving on the CB paradigm, NGOs do not want to lose it, and food-aid programs have integrated it in their standard package; of late, claims for perpetual subsidization (construed as exploiting the donor sensitivity to the "food security" argument).

Donor response. Due to Berg's and Kent's high professional standing and the mounting experience with failing projects, donors finally hesitant to consider further requests for CB support; instead, support for individual operators in the rural production/distribution system, potentially under joint liability group-credit arrangement, attracting growing interest.

2.2.2   History

Paradigmatic Background

The paradigmatic background favoring the emergence of "war on waste" programs as discussed above (case 1) is also at the root of the emergence of the CB model, that is, the concept of a chronically indebted, technologically backward, and food-insecure farming population at the mercy of unscrupulous speculators and moneylenders.

The CB ideology first appeared in the mid-1960s; donor-funded NGO programs entered in a massive way from the late 1970s on, a chronology quasi-parallel to the food-loss campaign. While PFL and related "war on waste" programs were predominantly geared to alleged technological deficiencies, the CBs concept showed particular concern for alleged merchant exploitation and food insecurity.

The term "cereal banks" or "grain banks" was first used in a comparison of monetary and grain-based security in a 1964 paper promoting the production and distribution of the "Waller village bin": "We accept the establishment and operation of banking systems . . . because we rightly attach great importance to the security of money . . . But consider the case of edible grains. They are far more important than money . . . And yet tens of millions of tons are permitted to go to waste every year . . . It is the purpose of these proposals to encourage the establishment of a system of small village 'banks' or stores throughout the grain producing areas."[69]

The first "banque de céréales" was probably that established in Kollo in Burkina Faso in 1974 (Ledoux 1987). In a paper written for the oldest national development agency in this country, Fonds National du Développement Economique et Social (FONADES, formerly FOVODES), the first CB created through this agency, apparently in conjunction with Oxford Committee on Famine Relief (Oxfam) and Cooperative for Assistance and Relief Everywhere (CARE), is (probably erroneously) dated back to 1964 (Dolidon 1980, 7).

---

69. W. Waller and A. C. Ross, "Proposal for Dispersed Grain Storage," Totnes, Devon, February 1964, 1, 2.

Spontaneous Collective Action?

While a number of CB enthusiasts nurse the idea that spontaneous collective action lay at the root of the movement, evidence of such is hard to find. In fact, it is ruled out by the following statement by FONADES, the generally acknowledged pioneer in the CBs arena: "Since the creation of the first cereal bank . . . FONADES has not modified its original concept which asks villagers to . . ." (Dolidon 1980, 7).

The external, "introduced" nature[70] of this "people's participation"/"grass-roots initiative" has prevailed throughout its history, as the account of its more recent donor-supported invasion (approximately 1,000 CB or rice-bank establishments, of which 400 are WFP-funded) into Laos confirms: "Although rice banks were regarded . . . a useful instrument to raise family food security, no permanent rice bank was found whose origin went back to the own initiative of the village population alone."[71] Considering the generally weak condition (faulty location, "poor state" of store construction and management, doubtful "cohesiveness among partners to run such an institution") of these "relatively young institutions," which do not "allow presently any conclusions about their sustainability," the report concludes: "The idea of establishing rice banks by the project was introduced at a stage of project formulation when little was known about the involvement of other organizations in this field of activity . . . In view of the involvement of already a large number of aid agencies in the establishment of village rice banks in the Lao [People's Democratic Republic], this project should not, as originally envisaged, start similar work well covered by other organizations" (7, 8, 10).

The Laotian case typifies the uncoordinated bandwagon sweep of the CBs ideology as a convenient outlet for donor funds, even in recent years when empirical analysis casting doubt on the model's sustainability has been available. The restraint advised by the 1993 FAO pilot-project report, however, may be seen as an indication of dwindling international confidence in CBs as a panacea.

The Ideology

The objectives of the CBs ideology have hardly changed, despite shifts in emphasis on the principal elements (marketing, food security, storage technology, social functions, and collective organization), lately emphasizing food security after other important elements proved unconvincing.

In 1980, the FOVODES viewpoint (which dated back to its first CBs in the early 1970s) was

---

70. In Niger, e.g., CBs in great numbers were simply imposed without awaiting villagers' requests ("90% des banques céréalières n'ont pas formulé (même) de demande en matière d'implantation de b.c." [Seyni Harouna, "Situation Actuelle des Banques Céréalières Implantés au Niger," FAO, Niamey and Rome, May 1990, 28]).

71. "Pilot Project for the Development of the National Food Security Program," Technical Working Paper no. 3, FAO/UNDP, Vientiane and Rome, August 1993, 6.

A [CB] can be defined as a village level organization for the marketing and storage of cereals, created by the villagers grouping themselves under a management committee.

A [CB] permits farmers to control for themselves, at village level, storage and marketing problems associated with their food crops.

In cutting out the traders the villagers can benefit from the profit margin normally realized by the middlemen in the same way that cooperative growers do.

In storing the grain at village level, the farmers have advance warning of cereal deficits, which can be severe at certain times.

Finally, in teaching villagers to manage grain stocks on a community basis FOVODES pursues an educational objective. (Dolidon 1980, 7)

FOVODES helped to realize these objectives by setting up a "management committee," providing material and professional construction inputs to build a store with a capacity of 25 tons, an initial stock of up to 30 tons covered by a grant, and providing "moral and legal support, training and advice" (7, 8). Soon the marketing element started to gain critical importance, since substantial, in part unforeseen, costs such as stock deterioration and other "disappearances" had to be covered by trading margins. Cutting out the alleged private "speculators" also proved attractive in mobilizing donor support ("Du stockage, elles sont passées à la commercialisation des produits provenant de ces réserves afin de lutter contre la 'spéculation' des commerçants privés. Une entreprise de justice, qui ne peut, pensent-ils, que plaire aux donateurs" [Thiéba 1992, 14]).

A paper commissioned by the Comité International pour la Lutte contre la Sécheresse au Sahel (CILSS) and OECD reduced its definition of a CB to "une organisation villageoise de stockage et de commercialisation des céréales" (Ledoux 1987, 7). The Berg and Kent (1991, 1) definition is similar, but includes dependence on outside assistance: "Village organizations that buy, store, and sell basic food grains . . . managed by a local village committee with the assistance of an international, government, or private voluntary agency." A workshop organized by CILSS, Bureau International du Travail (BIT), and FAO, the Atelier (October 1991), produced a confident, if not to say optimistic, definition: "une institution villageoise pour assurer les fonctions suivantes: a) la fonction sécurité alimentaire; b) commercialisation des céréales; c) l'accroissement des revenus des bénéficiaires; d) la régulation des prix céréaliers; e) l'augmentation de la productivité agricole" (FAO et al. 1992, 70).

A tone of reservation, however, entered the discussion when, at an international seminar in 1994, the GTZ representative "defined cereal banks as profitable (or at least cost-covering) local organizations which, by order of the local community, buy, store and sell grain and make a contribution to food security and rural development in selected areas," adding "that it is important to recognize, however, that . . . they cannot replace the private sector and they can never be used to store a significant stock of lasting food reserves."[72] One year later, a GTZ publication summarized the result of an extensive socioeconomic analysis: with very rare exceptions, CBs survive only as subsidized projects (Günther and Mück 1995, 34)!

The GTZ analysis confirmed that the extraordinarily tenacious CB ideology was breaking down. In the previous two decades, the ideology had attracted donor support for the establishment and operation of approximately 7,000 such village institutions, at an estimated average for aid-funds input of U.S.$30,000 (in 1995 dollars), that is, a total aid input of over $200 million.

Though the weaknesses of the ideology were apparent at an early stage, criticisms in scattered studies and project reports were not followed up seriously by the NGOs, development agencies, and donor institutions involved. The ideology was politically too attractive, providing too easy an outlet for donor funds earmarked for rural development as well as for accumulating food-aid stocks, and opening too "appropriate" an arena for expanding NGO activity, to be willingly subjected to unbiased evaluation.

After the collapse of cooperative systems in most developing countries, ardent proponents of collective enterprise transferred their hopes to the CBs movement. When states withdrew from direct market intervention, these proponents were joined by those who believed in "organized marketing," as against the allegedly inefficient and exploitative private traditional marketing activities.[73] Therefore, in spite of being highly vulnerable to market liberalization and the desubsidization policies of "structural adjustment," many CBs could prolong their existence due to the prolonged political, financial, material, and professional support generally available to them, until starting in the early 1990s socioeconomic realism gradually gained the upper hand.

Early Warnings

Already in the early 1980s reports on situations in Mali and Burkina Faso drew attention to the tendency of CBs to become monopolized by village

---

72. IFAD note on informal seminar among representatives of Australian Centre for International Agricultural Research, Centre International en Recherche Agronomique pour le Développement, FAO, GTZ, IFAD, and NRI, intervention by GTZ project director "für Nacherntefragen," Rome, June 1994, 2.

73. In addition to remarks on the dilemma of the intellectuals' (mis-)comprehension of the contribution to development by private trade (cf. section 2.2.1), two relevant comments on the viability of collectively (cooperative/village group) organized economic activities may be useful: (1) "The ability of groups to form and dissolve at short notice represents one of the strengths of the traditional system of cooperative enterprise, since it implies flexibility to adjust to changing circumstances. To attach great importance to promoting the permanence of project-sponsored groups is to ignore characteristics inherent in social organizations" (IFAD 1996, 24). (2) "It is often thought that government-supported cooperatives represent the best of both worlds in that they serve the public interest without the political and administrative difficulties presented by government operation. The truth seems to be rather the reverse. Such organizations are subject neither to the commercial or competitive test of the market nor to the public scrutiny to which government agents or corporations are sometimes exposed" (Bauer 1991, 90–91).

elites,[74] turning them "en une affaire privée."[75] Such monopolization was made the more attractive by the disproportionately high infusion of capital grants (often without even the organization of voluntary labor assistance in the construction of the village store [ibid.]), the negative real interest on loan funds, and the toleration of low loan-recovery rates (30–50%).[76]

These early reports identified the weakness of the "community" approach to the introduction and operation of entrepreneurial/technological innovations and the uncoordinated haste of a great number of organizations, mainly NGOs, in CB development, leading to, among other things, maintenance and spare-part problems because of unnecessary equipment diversity.[77] They also admitted the dependence on statutory (guaranteed) outlets for CB grain sales as well as procurement sources for inventory replenishment,[78] and grave problems in store construction and management, which caused high grain losses, mainly through pest infestation and humidity.[79]

The Gambia report, with reference to 12 Freedom from Hunger Campaign [FFHC]–supported CBs, argued:

> Such banks could not be economically self-sustaining, as they absorb too many scarce resources in relation to the quantities of grain they handle, in spite of the fact that other reports suggested that further banks should be built. However, a quarter of a million dollars has been spent on these banks so far to support them and in view of their present position further inputs are unlikely to make a drastic change in their situation . . . As a result of this experience . . . it is not advised that further bank programs are planned for the future.[80]

But at the time (mid-1980s) more such courageous arguments were necessary to put a brake on the CB boom and to redirect resources.

---

74. C. J. R. Roche, "Cereal Banks in Burkina Faso: A Case Study," Ouagadougou, 1984, 59; Rosalind Eyben, report on visit to Mali 83/003, FAO.

75. A. Diop, "Revue du Dessin, de la Construction, et des Opérations Techniques de Banque de Céréales en Haute-Volta," FAO, Rome, February 1983, ii.

76. E.g., Altarelli-Herzog, "Quelles Stratégies," 10; V. Altarelli-Herzog, "Promotion des Structures Villageoises Correspondantes," FAO, Rome and Ouagadougou, 1984, 40.

77. Altarelli-Herzog, "Quelles Stratégies," 10; Wanders and Antony, "Review of P. H. Technology," 20–21.

78. Altarelli-Herzog, "Promotion des Structures Villageoises Correspondantes," 44; Diop, "Revue du Dessin," v: "Compte tenu de difficultés éprouvées par plusieurs BC, soit pour écouler leurs céréales, soit pour s'approvisionner en temps voulu, il est recommendé à l'OFNACER [Office National de Céréales] d'utiliser toutes les possibilités offertes par les BC [banque de céréales] pour étendre ses activités de commercialisation et de distribution jusqu'au niveau du village."

79. Diop, "Revue du Dessin," 3–4.

80. Wanders and Antony, "Review of P. H. Technology," 19.

2.2.3   Neuralgic Points

Individual versus Collective Storage

Whereas the low quality of CB store management and resulting stock losses were gradually conceded in the mid-1980s, a widespread belief in much higher losses in farm household storage persisted. Failing to provide additional field-research information on this important aspect, project reports tended to reiter-ate insubstantial estimates and generalizations ("La plupart des contraintes et des pertes sont imputables au caractère rudimentaire des technologies de con-servation des récoltes" [rapp. PFL BKF/001, FAO (PFL), 1985, 1]).

Under a paradigm based on such alleged storage problems in the traditional system, in spite of research results proving that they were grossly exagger-ated,[81] the "eagerness" of villagers for a CB, as reported by enthusiastic pro-moters, was often more imagined than real ("Dans l'ensemble . . . l'édification de ces banques de céréales a répondu aux aspirations des groupements vil-lageois").[82] The fact that no CB had been the result of a spontaneous local initiative, that all were subsidized impositions, casts doubt on the significance of such self-flattering stereotypes. Moreover, a 1988/89 situation analysis on Mali[83] and Ledoux's observation of exchanges of unsold CB stocks against members' new crop "pour éviter les problèmes de conservation" (Ledoux 1988, 27) give a clear indication of the comparative advantage of traditional farm storage technology.

As unbiased field observation and research (e.g., Tyler and Bennet 1993, 27) confirm, villagers have a preference for maintaining food-security stocks in their individual and/or family stores ("Les paysans sont de l'avis que leurs structures d'entreposage sont assez adéquates"[84] and "For our food security, we prefer to take care of this each in his own granary"[85]). They also prefer to use natural pest-control agents (wood or banana-leaf ashes, mill dust, smoke, etc.) rather than the chemical insecticides necessary for bulk storage. Those and other local preferences contributed to the failure of CBs in Rwanda and Burkina Faso.[86] Their project designs and replication programs were not adapted to local realities ("ne [semblaient] pas tenir suffisamment en compte

---

81. Highlighted by Ledoux (1987, 10): "Si dans les années 70, on pensait que les pertes dues au stockage traditionnel pouvaient s'élever à 20–30% de la production, plusieurs études appro-fondies ont prouvé que les pertes attribuées au stockage paysan sont très faibles, de l'ordre de 5%."

82. J. Ramankatsoina, "Rapport du Mission 5–16 Juillet 1983," FAO, Ouagadougou and Rome, July 1983.

83. "Cereals in a Surplus Year: Some Thoughts on Mali 1988/89," mimeograph, Near East Foundation, Douentza, Mali, April 1989.

84. Altarelli-Herzog, "Quelles Stratégies," 34.

85. Personal communication with WFP staff, Rome, December 1993.

86. Altarelli-Herzog, "Quelles Stratégies," 8, 10, 23, 24.

les réalités sociales, économiques, institutionnelles et physiques du milieu dans lesquelles les projets doivent se dérouler").[87]

The Village-Store Panacea

In Tanzania, where by 1991, with the help of "UNDP, FAO, EEC, USAID, CIDA [Canadian International Development Agency], CDTF [Commonwealth Development Trust Fund], GTZ, and others, a total of 926 stores had been constructed" since the launching of the government's Village Store Construction Project, "it became apparent towards the end of the project that many village stores were not fully utilized by the villagers," that in fact they "remained empty for most of the year," and that "the grains found in the village stores belonged to the Union, the government-owned NMC [National Milling Corporation] or Breweries (in Segese 1600 bags of paddy belonged to a private trader)." In summary, "the villagers have not utilized the stores for their own food security." Obviously, "villagers in the country seemed reluctant to store surplus produce in the Village Stores," mentioning "lack of confidence in public management," "inconvenience," and "lack of direct control of their property . . . among the reasons for preferring household storage."[88]

These observations were confirmed and expanded by NRI staff reports on Tanzania (Coulter 1994) and Zambia (Tyler and Bennet 1993), that is, that small farmers prefer to store in their farmstead or household compound, that their storage losses are inferior to those observed in collective storage, that no capacity constraints are felt in their (traditional) storage facilities,[89] that even after decline or collapse of parastatal grain-marketing institutions they did not suffer serious marketing problems in a general environment of competitive, low-profit rural grain trade.

Why, then, this rush of donors and development agencies to support a village-store project in Tanzania, a country with extraordinary overcapacity, of approximately 200% (Coulter and Golob 1992) in collective (mainly public and cooperative) grain-storage facilities?

Traditional Food Security

Knowledge of traditional food-security systems was available, for example, Diop's reference to farmers' grain reserves (1983), "parfois jusqu'à 2 ou 3 années de consommation familiales,"[90] or Ledoux's account (1987, 5) of family grain reserves enough for several years of drought in succession: "En plus du stock annuel qui permet à la famille de se nourrir entre une récolte et la suivante, il est nécessaire de constituer des stocks pluriannuelles pour le cas où

---

87. Ibid., 25, 29.

88. Hauli and Kidunda, "Role of Village Stores," 2, 14, 35, 26.

89. "No concern" was expressed by Tanzanian small farmers at the prospect of a bumper crop to store, "except that a bumper crop would result in less theft" (Coulter and Golob 1991, 45).

90. Diop, "Revue du Dessin," 1.

la récolte serait insuffisante . . . Traditionnellement un célibataire s'honorait de disposer de 4 à 5 années de réserves pour prétendre au mariage."

Guggenheim (1991, 109, 129) provided an excellent account of the elaborate extended-family granary system in Dogon (Mali) society, including the highly efficient quality-control system applied to the grain before and during storage, resulting in only 2–4% annual loss. Ample literature was available on traditional social organization of work parties, mutual assistance, social support, and environmental control.

But all this was overlooked by the CB promoters, fixated by their paradigm: "Il faut essayer de créer une certaine dynamique 'grenier de prévoyance': c'est-à-dire, qu'avoir son grenier, de plus en plus grand, devienne une mode pour les villages et qu'il y ait ainsi émolution."[91] The approach remained optimistic and uniform, as if in a vacuum, disregarding the density and diversity of the traditional systems summarized so aptly in a socioeconomic study: "les pratiques et les méthodes traditionnelles après-production sont multiformes et très développées."[92]

The Role of Food Aid

The role of food aid in setting in motion and accelerating the CB boom is discussed by Ledoux (1987). After the prolonged drought in the early 1970s, food aid tended to become a continuum that villagers learned to integrate into their storage strategy, and that initiated a shift of responsibility for food security from local (family, clan) systems toward collective and state-supported systems, including CB creations.

While the speculation on food-aid arrivals might not have been a decisive factor in farmers' reserve-stock policy, the CB device certainly served food-aid organizations as an outlet for surplus stocks or funds. The assistance Oxfam gave FOVODES in launching the first known CB program (1974), as well as the massive invasion of WFP-created CBs in Laos (1993) ("All of the permanent rice banks . . . have been set up exclusively with outside capital in the form of rice"),[93] and Harouna's observations (1990) on CB implantation in Niger[94] all seem to indicate this relationship.

It can also be assumed that many CBs with shrinking capital were given repeated food-aid allocations to recharge their stocks. The trend toward continued reliance on aid implanted in the CB institution was reinforced by the fact that its initial capital endowment and the storage facility were given more or less as a grant. Pointing to this trend, Koité deplored the disincentive effect this, and especially the access to restocking from aid, had on the obvious need

91. Report on CB program in Mali supported by Compagnie Malienne pour le Développement du Textile (CMDT) and SNV, a major Dutch NGO, around 1990 (cover page missing, presumably written for SNV, Bamako).

92. Altarelli-Herzog, "Quelles Stratégies," iii, referring to Rwanda and Burkina Faso.

93. "Pilot Project," 7.

94. Harouna, "Situation Actuelle."

to improve CB management performance ("le dynamisme insuffisant des comités de gestion qui comptent dans une certaine mesure sur l'assistance des projets pour les aider à reconstituer leur stocks").[95] Ledoux (1988, 27) discusses this problem ("des pertes significatives . . . partiellement compensées par la fourniture d'aide alimentaire gratuite qui a permis de reconstituer les stocks"; similarly, Bédouin: "De plus, certaines de ces BC ont bénéficié de plusieurs dotations depuis leur implantation").[96]

One can assume that food-aid surpluses put pressure on the CB system as an additional outlet. In the food-aid history of one Sahel country, for instance, in only one year (1990/91) of the five-year period 1989–1994 were food-aid deliveries in line with assessed "supply gap" needs; in the other four years there was an oversupply of 300% and more.[97] This kind of pressure is reflected in a field report from Sudan, where a number of FAO-established CBs, expecting negotiated initial grain stocks totaling 660 tons as starting capital, were suddenly confronted with an unannounced EEC donation of an additional 1,000 tons, jeopardizing the project's policy on sustainable CB management principles.[98]

The Forced-Sales Paradigm

The stereotypical argument that CBs protect poor farmers from exploitation through "forced or distress sales," that is, premature depletion of their harvested grain stocks due to indebtedness (mainly to traders), which necessitates grain purchases at increased prices later in the season, is no longer defensible. Already in 1986 a CILSS analysis of "recent" research reports observed that this paradigm lacked foundation ("qu'il n'y a aucun signe prouvant que les petits cultivateurs les plus pauvres sont ceux-là qui se trouvent dans l'obligation de vendre et de racheter ensuite") and that peasants do spread their crop sales and take advantage of price fluctuations, preferring to sell other assets (including labor) for urgently needed cash.

---

95. C. Koité, "Rapport d'Evaluation" (Mauritania), MAU 92/006, FAO, Rome, June 1993, 10. That "food aid fosters dependency" has been widely recognized and criticized, e.g., with exceptional publicity by a courageous Oxfam official (Tony Jackson), adding that it "competes with local crops for customers and handling and storage facilities, is expensive to administer, often does not reach those in need and actually does more harm than good" (Oxfam 1982, 57). Others, apart from unanimously referring to its "disincentive effects on local food production," claim that it "generated extremely expensive subsidy programs, created administrative nightmares, and encouraged corruption" (Gallarotti 1991, 201–2; Hopkins 1992).

96. R. Sauvinet-Bédouin, "Rapport Technique: Contribution à l'Evaluation à Mi-Parcours du Projet Burkina Faso 3326/1 (WFP): Développement Rural," FAO/Food Security Service and WFP, Rome, 1996, 8.

97. "Flux d'Aide Alimentaire Destinée aux Pays du CILSS," WFP working paper, 1994, cited by Günther and Mück 1995, 62.

98. T. Long, "Food Grain Storage/Food Grain Banks, Kordofan State, Sudan," project report, SUD/87/008, FAO, Karthoum and Rome, December 1992, 3.

Les ventes ont lieu toute l'année même si les cultivateurs qui cherchent uniquement à vendre préfèrent le faire pendant la période de disette! Ceci ne correspond pas à l'image traditionnelle, dans la mesure où l'on suggère ainsi que les cultivateurs sont tout à la fois désireux et capables de bénéficier des fluctuations saisonnières des prix . . . [To cover pressing cash needs] les petits exploitants ont effectivement certaines alternatives à la vente de leurs céréales; l'une des plus importantes étant de travailler hors de l'exploitation. (CILSS 1986, 14–15)

The Revolving Credit-in-Kind Model

In Mali, where Dutch-funded programs, among others, had emphasized the credit-in-kind business as the principal engine for CB promotion ("la plus significative de la possibilité d'une capitalisation à partir des céréales"),[99] Belloncle found a disastrous situation of indebtedness ("une situation catastrophique du point de vue des remboursements internes et externes . . . on imagine le 'choc' qu'a pu constituer la découverte de la situation réelle!" [i.e., an average recovery rate of only 30%, established with difficulty due to "l'absence totale de documents de gestion fiables"]).[100]

The problem of low repayment rates is aggravated by the observation that they decline with the age of a CB, "ce qui nous amène à parler de solidarisation à rebours dans le non payement des crédits internes."[101] Apart from capital shrinkage caused by bad debtors, there are further losses as turnover falls because bad debtors are refused further credit and other members' demand for credit shrinks in response to tighter repayment conditions. In this desperate situation aging stocks have to be cleared on give-away terms of credit ("beaucoup de greniers pour renouveler leurs stocks ont effectué des placements sans intérêt" [32]).

Koldenhof and Diarra further expanded on the credit problem: a "taux d'intérêt de 50%" is observed; "non-remboursement" leading to "restrictions des prêts aux villageois"; shrinking and very irregular credit demand inviting "le problème d'écoulement" (e.g., "détérioration de 500 kg à Souara"); complaints about favoritism in the selection of credit receivers at give-away rates; and toleration of nonrepayment.[102] An interesting observation in this report is

---

99. Lending food or cash to members against repayment in kind at harvest time ought to have yielded substantial annual capital gains ("Le mouvement des crédits internes est la principale source de croissance des stocks des greniers de prévoyance . . . permettant une croissance brute théorique des stocks de 30 à 50% par an" (Paul van Wijk, projet de Greniers de Prévoyance, rapport bilan "Deuxième Campagne 1989–90," San, Mali, 1990, 29).

100. Guy Belloncle, "Associations Villageoises et Développement Rural Equilibré dans le Projet Mali Sud," Bamako, April 1990, 33, 34.

101. Van Wijk, "Deuxieme Campagne," 31.

102. E. Koldenhof and P. Diarra, "Le Fonctionnement des Banques de Céréales: Le Cas des Greniers de Prévoyance et Leur Adoption par Zone Ethnique et Agro-climatique," CMDT Direction Régional San (Mali), projet Greniers de Prévoyance, July 1991, 20–23.

the negative effect that grain available on easy credit terms had on labor supply (a crucial factor during the cultivation season), the easy access to food
removing the need to sell labor ("En plaçant le grain à tous les nécessiteux, ces
derniers ne sont plus obligés de travailler dans les champs d'autruis pour le
grain" [19]). This report also identifies the disastrous collapse of credit-in-
kind-based CBs in the face of a "solidarité à rebours" among the indebted
population (e.g., "sous prétexte de mauvaises récoltes"): "Ceux qui peuvent
rembourser vont imiter les plus démunis qui ne le peuvent pas" (87).[103] The
authors present a convincing model of the counterproductive effect of the
credit-based CB (73).[104]

An annex report on the situation of a CB in a food-deficit region in Mali offered a thoughtful conclusion: if there were a solution to the problem of food
security, the peasants themselves would have discovered it ("Après tout," for
the "problème de la sécurité alimentaire . . . il n'y a pas de solutions évidentes,
sinon on peut supposer qu'il y a déjà longtemps que les paysans les auraient
découvertes [sic]).[105]

---

103. That this situation in Mali represents a general malaise is confirmed by a more recent
evaluation report on a major program promoting group credit (including a CB type of inventory
credit) in Anglophone West Africa: "NGOs/line agencies initiated groups with the ultimate
purpose of acquiring credit . . . too much emphasis on receiving credit (in cash or kind) and haste
of NGOs in reaching the targeted number of groups [were among] main factors which reduced
group effectiveness . . . increased the incidence of group dispersion and unsustainability after
receiving the credit . . . [and] low level of servicing and repayments of loans . . . so far, groups
have not evolved into cost-effective units . . . overall, they lacked cohesion and sustainability"
(IFAD 1996, 11, 15).

104. "Conséquences des mauvaises récoltes

| | | [conséquence] | |
	[réaction]	[individuelle]	[cumulative]
[première phase]	Crainte (par le comité) d'une éventuelle incapacité de remboursement. Nombre élevé des gens qui ont peur de ne pas pouvoir rembourser leur crédit.	Limitation de la quantité prise.	[déclin progressif du chiffre d'affair de la banque céréale]
[seconde phase]	Nombre élevé des débiteurs qui sont exclus d'un nouveau emprunt.	Diminution du nombre des gens qui empruntent.	

Vus les pourcentages des exploitations qui empruntent le mil et les quantités prises en rapport
avec le besoin élevé, la contribution du GP à la sécurité est faible" (Koldenhof and Diarra, "Le
Fonctionnement des Banques de Céréales," 73; completed by the author for easier comprehension). GP means grenier de prévoyance, used here as a synonym for banque de céréales or cereal
bank.

105. Annex 2 (to an unidentified report), "La banque de céréale de Poye," n.d., 12.

Bandwagon Chaos

Harouna's summary of weaknesses of the CB program in Niger is indicative of implementation problems in the bandwagon competition for donor funds and projects:[106]

- Ninety-five percent of the "banks" were placed in a relatively wealthy agricultural zone, where crop variety and cash crop income provide sufficient basis for individual food security.
- Ninety percent were not requested by the villagers.
- In most cases, the arrival of the initial grain stock took the beneficiaries by surprise.
- Uncoordinated donor activity led to duplication of CB creations in villages, even those with a history of CB failure.
- At 98% of the visited CBs, "le niveau des comités de gestion laisse à désirer."
- In most cases, CB management was dominated by a privileged minority: "Les diverses fonctions coopératives sont assumées par les même clans familiaux."
- The great majority of the population perceived the CB as a public or donor-controlled entity,[107] which left little hope for a self-supporting future, while "subsidization cannot go on indefinitely and in fact might dry out soon."
- Excessive paternalism marked the attitude of external promoters and organizers.
- Storage facilities were deficient.
- As for the inability of the banks to trade at a sufficient margin to cover even operational costs, not to speak of remuneration for management inputs, management committees disintegrated as they lacked the means to compensate members for their participation.
- With regard to the banks' advised policy of earning substantial trade profits on loans in kind to members, this has contributed to rural indebtedness ("L'endettement des populations rurales ne pourra pas résoudre le problème de sécurité alimentaire").
- In conclusion, the CB paradigm presents an unsuitable model for the subregion ("Au terme de ce bref survol de la problématique liée au développement des banques céréales, il serait temps d'abandonner certaines méthodes d'intervention en milieu rural qui semblent être un placage ou une reproduction d'expériences vécues ailleurs dans la sous-région").

---

106. Harouna, "Situation Actuelle," 27–31.

107. This observation was shared by Koldenhof and Diarra ("Le Fonctionnement des Banques de Céréales," 55): "Malgré l'arrivée du Projet Greniers de Prévoyance" the "bancs," created three years earlier through "l'aide en nature octroyé," still are "considérée comme une aide pendant la période de soudure plutôt qu'une école d'autopromotion."

Associations ex Nihilo

Against this background, the artificiality of the CB movement became more and more apparent, as a socioeconomic consultant report on the situation in Sierra Leone highlighted.[108] The report points at the heterogeneity of a rural settlement: "There are wide ranges of variations in dependency ratios, farmer output, income derivations, support of relatives living elsewhere, and indebtedness. These variations tend to be the main reasons for individualism and needs among rural farmers" (22). "Storage has always been a single household unit affair. Like a bank account, the status of the food store is a confidential matter and sometimes highly personalised" (14–15). "The relatively 'youthful' status of farmer groups has been rendered possible through surviving agricultural development packages" from the time when "most of the country was until recently festooned with Integrated Agricultural Development projects" (13, 15). "It is difficult to find a justification for delivery of the quality of storage proposed to any of the present associations . . . They see these new stores as facilities that can be sublet, rented to traders and travellers and used for keeping products from group farm activities." Past experience warns, the report argues, "that these stores do not revert to one-man enterprises," as has been the tendency in the past and more so today, after "rural communities have lost the drive for group formation" (12–14, 19).

The latter was confirmed by the experience of a member of the PRMC donor committee:[109] "In my travel through Sahel countries I have met not one CB that was free of serious problems." In one village, however, he met a happy congregation: the village CB had been dissolved; a good harvest had permitted payment of debts, and it was decided to discontinue the activity. As a member of the dissolved management committee explained: "For our food security, we prefer to take care of this each in his own granary!"—PRMC was among the first donor institutions that decided to withdraw CB support.

Thiéba (1992) was much sharper in his criticism of the artificial creation of what he calls "associations des producteurs 'ex nihilo' " and of the role of NGOs in this activity: in contrast with the "true" forms of communal organization based on traditional systems of mutual support and solidarity, these new "associations villageois" such as CBs are paper creations, thriving on the uninformed sympathy of the aid system, the "manne extérieure." Their activity is concentrated on the lobby for aid, which tends to profit a strategic clique and in the final analysis serves consumption rather than production. They destabilize rather than strengthen communal solidarity.[110]

---

108. Harry Turay, "The Improvement of Crop Post-harvest Practices at the Village Level," Njala University College, Sierra Leone, January 1990.

109. Personal communication with WFP staff, Rome, December 1993.

110. "Mais ces groupements sont'ils des vraies organisations paysannes qui fonctionnent selon les formes traditionnelles de solidarité villageoise? En sont-ils des émanations désignées selon un mode de délégation volontaire du pouvoir? En fait, ces associations ne sont pas issues

By the early 1990s there were still many supporters of the CBs model, who in spite of its introduced, heavily subsidized, and therefore largely artificial nature tried to justify its continued support, for example with Ledoux's 1986 explanation: "La banque de céréales est un élément qui participe et facilite le passage d'une économie de subsistance à une économie du marché"; or with FAO's hope to create CBs as "des moyens efficaces pour redynamiser le secteur coopératif rural et la participation paysanne au développement national";[111] or backed by African politicians who had used the model as an important element in their rural campaigning for many years, and, most ardently, by NGO cadres committed to CB programs.

Some African professionals, on the other hand, had begun to oppose models tied to unending dependence on aid. They had also become increasingly sensitive to interventions that aimed to change the social fabric of their rural ecology, as demonstrated by statements of African researchers, consultants, and civil servants quoted in this study.[112]

2.2.4   Refuge in Defiance? The Case of Country X

Background

The overall picture of the CB movement in the late 1980s was one of fast, though fragmentary and uncoordinated, expansion of national programs. This was particularly true in countries with a relatively recent CB history (e.g., Niger, Laos, Tanzania), willingly supported by the donor community via eager NGOs, technical-assistance agencies, food-aid and development-financing

---

d'un combat politique ou économique commun, et ne sont pas non plus à l'origine d'un projet de société villageois. Elles rencontrent pourtant un réel succès en France auprès des réseaux d'aide au développement, et cette manne extérieure les amène à se détourner parfois de leurs objectives initiaux. Aucun contrôle réel n'est effectué sur la répartition des subventions reçues. Les 'leaders' associatifs se reconvertissent ainsi dans la recherche exclusive des fonds et utilisent parfois ces sommes pour une gestion clientéliste des rapports de pouvoir dans l'association . . . Car en encourageant des 'associations' qui n'ont que le nom de villageois, ils ont favorisé l'ancrage de pareils comportements. L'aide qu'ils ont fournie n'est plus consommée que ponctuellement, pour être attendue à nouveau, et êtres aussitôt consommée . . . Dans ces conditions, elle ne peut jouer qu'un rôle démobilisateur, les groupements proposant volontairement des prix très élevés aux clients afin de satisfaire l'appétit de leurs membres . . . Les opérations de commercialisation menées par des associations de producteurs crées *ex nihilo* ont prouvé leur inefficience. Les intentions de départ ont été sévèrement sanctionnées par le marché et les stratégies des prétendus bénéficiaires. Elles n'ont pas été capables de mettre en place une troisième voie entre le 'tout marché' et le 'tout Etat' " (Thiéba 1992, 14–16).

111. Project document MAU/92/006, FAO, Rome, 1992, 11.

112. Diop, "Revue du Dessin"; Koité, "Rapport d'Evaluation"; Intervention par le Directeur National du Projet Banques de Céréales en Pays X (M. Nyang) in proceedings of FAO/GASGA seminar, L'Expérience Africaine en Amélioration des Techniques Post-Récolte, Accra, July 1994; Koldenhof and Diarra, "Le Fonctionnement des Banques de Céréales"; Harouna, "Situation Actuelle"; Hauli and Kidunda, "Role of Village Stores"; Turay, "Improvement of Crop Post-harvest Practices"; and Thiéba 1992.

institutions, despite rising awareness of serious defects in the movement's institutional viability and the basic paradigm underpinning its ideology.

Much of the expansion had taken place by replicating existing programs in a process of refuge in defiance, similar to processes observed in food-loss-prevention programs described in case 1 (section 2.1.3). Differentiation between first-, second-, and third-generation projects had become fashionable, and the follow-up project in the sequence was almost invariably committed to restoring the inherited, often dormant, CBs established by its predecessor(s), with a general tendency to increase the scale of the program.

CB history in country X, a latecomer on the CB bandwagon, reflects this trend.

Program Evolution and Investment

The CB movement entered country X relatively late and on a modest scale, as a series of three projects, the first two bilaterally and the third multilaterally funded. Together they covered the period 1984–96.

Each project, before its termination, generated a proposal for a follow-up project. However, the lengthy process of reaching agreement between the three partners, that is, donor, government, and executing agency, and the additional lead time until project implementation, caused unintended breaks (of approximately two years each) in monitoring and support of the newly established CBs, which a badly equipped government counterpart service was unable to bridge.[113]

The first project established 5 banks, the second added 10, and the third aimed to complete another 12. The modest rates of sequential increase were related to the failure of the second project to establish more than half of the originally planned 20 new banks. This fact, together with other problems of the second project, induced a more cautious approach in the third project proposal. The government's financial commitment also dropped to the extraordinary low level of only 2.5% of total funding for the third project,[114] while the 15% contribution for the second project had been within the normal range of receiver government support for aid projects.

Of the total funding input of about U.S.$2.5 million for the three projects—of which 60% was for the third project alone—at least half,[115] that is, nearly $50,000 per bank, was for establishing and monitoring the 27 CBs.[116] This

---

113. "Rapport d'Evaluation des Banques de Céréales," project 03, June 1993, 15; "Rapport de Mission d'Appui Technique au Projet 03," April 1993, 12, 13; "Rapport Term. Projet 02," June 1990, 11, 12, 23.

114. Project document 03, signed 12 July 1992, cover page.

115. The remainder related to other project components.

116. In the final analysis, this number needs to be reduced, as the third project's CB creations fell short of the target by approximately 50%, resulting in an even higher overall average investment per bank.

does not include the postproject extended support (from government, NGO, and food-aid agency) received by these banks.

Replication, Revitalization, and Monitoring

Partly due to problems encountered in delivering the initial grain stock at the agreed (and seasonally appropriate) time,[117] neither of the first two projects could witness its newly established CBs in operation over a full crop cycle. Nevertheless, evaluation missions, terminal project reports, and project documents reiterated confidence in their viability and in the desirability of their replication.[118]

No postproject evaluation was implemented before finalization of the successor (second [BC2] or third [BC3] "generation") project document, although the two-year interval would surely have provided ample data for an evaluation of the operational performance of the banks. Instead, a commitment to evaluate, monitor, and rehabilitate the CB creations of their predecessors was a major component of the work program of the new projects.

However, realization of this component lagged far behind expectations. Project 02, already 50% short of its CB construction program, proved equally deficient in rehabilitating, monitoring, and assisting with the five first-generation CBs left two years earlier by project 01: "De son côté l'équipe du projet a effectué seulement une dizaine de missions de suivi [*sic*]. Pendant la première année, les membres du projet étaient très pris par la construction et la formation des comités de gestion des BC2. En plus, l'éloignement des BC1 (du nouveau siège du projet) a mené à une fréquence de suivi qui était insuffisante."[119]

How unproductive such monitoring visits can be is highlighted in a report by the field-project manager of the third-generation project (03) on his "mission de suivi" under the project's "objectif du suivi, de la réhabilitation et du renforcement des BC existantes" (i.e., five first-generation CBs and ten second-generation CBs). In spite of sending out questionnaires in advance and traveling extensively over a two-month period, in most cases the mission neither met relevant committee members nor obtained financial and commercial accounts that would have enabled them to assess the operational history and the current financial situation of the banks: "Cette évaluation ne se voit donc pas exhaustive du fait que la mission n'a pu accéder à certains documents, notamment ceux ayant trait à la gestion, pour cause d'absence de détenteurs de ces documents."[120]

---

117. Cf. project 02. This is a common problem, particularly with locally procured aid components.

118. See, e.g., project document 03, 3, commenting on the CBs established by project 02 in 1989: "Il n'a pas encore d'étude sur l'impact de l'opération mais la demande est forte."

119. "Rapport Term. Projet 02," 13.

120. "Rapport d'Evaluation" (des renseignements du "mission de suivi"), June 1993, 1.

Persistent Problems

Nevertheless, these visits uncovered the extremely problematic position of these banks. Some had still not established a "comité de gestion"; in others, "aucune opération n'avait été réalisée depuis deux campagnes"; and yet others were found to be deadlocked ("bloqué à cause de problèmes internes à la communauté villageoise").[121] The general impression was one of "un dés-intérêt de certaines franges de ces populations dont les femmes et les jeunes pour les Banques de Céréales," that "il n'a pas d'approbation de la Banque par les communautés villageoises" (3, 5).

Summarizing the situation on the basis of a number of visits to second-generation CBs, a "rapport de mission d'appui technique" (April 1993, 1) identified "décapitalisation (leurs stocks actuels sont réduits presque à la moitié); infrastructures déficientes: larges fissures dans les parois; conflit entre objectif commercial et social."

In spite of energetic attempts to improve the situation by the field-project manager—who was increasingly tied down by the problems in constructing and operationalizing his newly established 12 third-generation CBs, a major part of *his* project—a consultant mission report ten months later concluded: "Malgré certaines améliorations on relève encore des faiblesses au niveau de l'enregistrement comptable, de l'hygiène du magasin, de l'entretien et de la protection des stocks et de la commercialisation."[122]

Regarding the donors' concerns about the problematic state of the CB pro-gram, it should be noted that at the end of the second project "le donateur n'a pas envoyé de participant à la mission tripartite";[123] that is, the only mission report that could influence the direction of the program became a quasi auto-evaluation by the two parties directly responsible for, and therefore protective about, the project results.

Cooperative Status?

The legal status of CBs in country X was that of "groupement précooperatif." This status might be converted to a cooperative, thus opening access to formal commercial and financing channels, after two years at the earliest, if a CB provides significant demonstration of its economic viability.

Deprived of statutory outlets for carryover stocks and facing a decline in the high subsidization rate of their rolling stock and working capital provision because of structural-adjustment/market-liberalization measures (introduced late in country X) and shrinking donor commitment, CBs could not be ex-pected to meet this condition. The comparative disadvantages in competition with rural grain trade and farm-storage efficiency,[124] and the lack of commu-

---

121. Ibid., 2.

122. "Rapport de Mission Projet BC (03)," February 1994, 30.

123. "Rapport Term. Projet 03," 10.

124. Clearly identified (ibid., 32).

nity commitment to compensate for these disadvantages, ruled out this possibility.

New Political Climate

The political climate in country X, and in development agencies involved in the program, started to change, however, which affected the CB ideology and its underlying paradigm. While the project document 03 of July 1992 still reiterated classic cooperative arguments, for example that "les villageois veulent se libérer des mouvements spéculatifs des commerçants" (8) and "des crédits usuraires qui hypothèquent les récoltes à venir" (12), the "rapport de mission d'appui technique" of April 1993 defined as a major term of reference of a scheduled consultant input "d'identifier les justifications des critiques actuelles dont sont victimes les commerçants" (3). The same report recommended "une politique de prix plus rationelle," for example, "adoption d'un prix *variable,* en fonction du prix de marché," while the project document 03 still based its economic-policy alignment on rather outdated national development plans for the periods 1985–88 and 1989–91, "accordant une priorité aux actions visant [à la] fixation des prix rémunérateurs aux paysans" (21).

The project's commitment to the "création d'une cellule nationale-Banques de Céréales" (project document 03, 13) within the Ministry of Rural Development, as an institution "assumant son rôle et développer ses activités à d'autres régions du pays, d'une manière autonome," has to be seen against this background. Together with this institutional innovation, a legal consultancy "pour la révision de la législation nécessaire . . . en vue de la mise en œuvre effective de la stratégie nationale de banques de céréales"[125] had been integrated into the project work plan. Combined, these targets seemed to indicate a wish to bypass the selection criteria of the cooperative law (economic viability, accounting discipline, etc.) and to legalize the program's unilateral access to preferential funding and subsidization.

Indicative of the new climate, however, a government decision in early 1993 "de suprimer toutes les 'Cellules' "[126] curtailed the optimistic assumptions of these propositions. Apparently, a new sense of independence based on the principle of sustainability had taken root among government and academic cadres. An African delegate to an international seminar on postharvest systems development evinced this with surprising frankness when he questioned the viability of the CB model with its heavy dependence on donor support and the salesmanlike approach of its promoters.[127]

---

125. "Rapport de Mission d'Appui Technique," April 1993, annex 7, containing the full terms of reference for such a consultancy.

126. Ibid., 1. A member of a 1995 evaluation mission ("Rapport d'Evaluation," FENU, April 1995) speaks of the "réticence des autorités (gouvernementales) à créer des cellules devant se substituer aux projets à la fin de ceux-ci."

127. "La viabilité du program de banques de céréales [dans mon pays] a été mise en doute, puisqu'il dépend pour les deux tiers de la contribution financière du projet. N'y a-t-il pas un

Inconclusive Halt

In early 1995, project 03 was halted by the funding partners' reluctance to provide further support for the project. The poorly manned midterm evaluation, scheduled to deliver an "exhaustive"[128] analysis of the situation, presented a slender and inconclusive report. It again stressed the chronic weaknesses of the project's predecessors: "Les réhabilitations prévues n'ont pas été entreprises, priorité ayant accordée à la construction, aujourd'hui aboutie, de six nouvelles banques. La mission n'a été en mesure que de procéder à une analyse très partielle, et peu satisfaisante, des indicateurs de performance BC." The mission failed ("n'a pas jugé devoir revenir dans le présent rapport") to discuss "les difficultés conceptionelles rencontrées au cours d'exécution du . . . projet."[129]

The question of the economic and social viability of the established (first-, second-, and third-generation) CBs remained unanswered. Instead, an accompanying "note" requested the use of CBs in food-aid distribution as a means of ensuring their survival ("à ce stade, il paraît essentiel de souligner l'importance s'attachant à l'engagement de l'Etat à canaliser l'aide alimentaire via les BC fiables et les futures unions régionales").[130]

According to more recent information, none of the CBs created by the three projects is still in operation.[131]

2.2.5   Policy Dilemma

The Major Comprehensive Evaluation Attempts (1990–95)

The early 1990s produced a number of analytical reports that were relevant to CB support policies.[132] These strengthened the intellectual basis for reconsideration and concentration of CB programs and, in a growing number of cases, withdrawal of further support.

The conceptual cornerstone of these reports was the Berg and Kent report (March 1991). Its excellent, courageous, and logical attack on deeply ingrained paradigms is comparable (at the macroeconomic level) to the structural-adjustment initiative of IMF/World Bank economists some years earlier. Like the initial response to that initiative, the response by professional

---

risque que le résultat ultime de tels programs soit plus que 'concret,' c'est-à-dire des monuments de métal et de briques à des projets échoués? Est-ce une façon de forcer les paysans au changement, de sorte que le personnel de vulgarisation devienne seulement des 'vendeurs' de nouvelles technologies?" (Intervention [Nyang], 34).

128. Project document 03, 14.

129. "Rapport d'Evaluation," FENU, i–iv.

130. Ibid., "Note," 2.

131. Personal communication with returning FAO/Investment Centre mission, June 1998.

132. FAO 1990; DAI, Berg and Kent 1991; FAO et al. 1992; and GTZ, Günther and Mück 1995.

colleagues and development workers devoted to the CB movement to the Berg and Kent report was defensive, disqualifying, or intentionally indifferent.

The report fueled some rethinking, however, and a number of donors scaled down their commitments. While the FAO Evaluation (October 1990), despite some realistic analysis, jeopardized the effect of its findings by reverting to politically adaptive conclusions, the Atelier (October 1991), convened after the publication of the Berg and Kent report, was considerably less concilia- tory, narrowing the path of feasible CB operation to a fraction of its former scope. Four years later, the GTZ study (October 1995) finally confirmed the Berg and Kent verdict: CBs were unsustainable without heavy, continuous subsidization (60).

Berg and Kent (1991) fractured the political aura that surrounded the CB ideology:

> Our first conclusion is that many of the assumptions that serve as ratio- nales for the involvement of CBs in grain marketing are analytically un- sound and empirically weak . . . [CBs are a] magnet for foreign aid . . . They have tremendous financial (or nominal) cost advantages over pri- vate traders, because of the large subsidies they receive . . . The avail- ability of these subsidies and the encouragement by donors and govern- ments that they reflect explain the existence of cereal banks . . . This popularity can be attributed to government and donor reticence to let market forces completely control cereal markets. (73–74)

> Cereal banks exhibit a quasi-general inability to cover operating costs, a rapid decline in activity as they mature, and a high mortality rate . . . de- spite the tremendous cost advantages . . . due mainly to subsidization by external aid agencies . . . Because of the magnitude of the resources that have been devoted to creating and nurturing CBs, these results have to be regarded as nothing less than disastrous. (52)

It is interesting to note that the conclusions of an earlier study for CILSS pointed in a similar direction (Houghton 1985).[133] The criticism in this study had much less effect on aid policy, because of its less provocative tone (the CB discussion was a minor component of a more comprehensive subsector analysis), its lower profile, and its timing: donors were not yet ready for criti- cal analysis.

Thus, while the FAO Evaluation still maintained that "[l]es banques de céréales peuvent jouer un rôle positif dans tous les cas, mais leur utilité est maximale dans les zones à équilibre précaire" (only that "le taux de succès et la viabilité de ces banques peuvent être améliorés, à la lumière de l'expérience passée, par un encadrement adapté" [FAO et al. 1992, 35]), a year later the

---

133. The CB section is cited as "the most systematic discussion" so far on the subject (Berg and Kent 1991, 3).

Atelier summary by the same key consultant who served on the evaluation team concludes:

> Les différentes évaluations faites au cours de ces dernières années soulignent toutes un taux d'échec assez élevé, ainsi qu'un taux de survie des BC relativement faible, une fois le projet de soutien retiré.
>
> Alors que dans la période précédente on avait souvent tendance à voir dans les BC une panacée pour résoudre le problème de sécurité alimentaire et de commercialisation des céréales, il apparaît désormais clairement que certaines fonctions ne peuvent être remplies par les banques:
>
> - les BC ne peuvent pas jouer une fonction d'aide sociale vis-à-vis des populations les plus défavorisées;
> - les BC ne sont pas la solution pour assurer un débouché stable et rémunérateur aux zones de production excédentaire;
> - les BC ne peuvent pas assurer une régulation interannuelle des marchés céréaliers en cas de récolte excédentaire, sauf à être soutenues par des mécanismes régulateurs à l'échelle nationale;
> - enfin les Banques ne peuvent pas, dans des conditions de concurrence équitable, se substituer au commerce privé, dont la fonction principale est l'approvisionnement des centres de consommation à partir des régions excédentaires. (37–38)

The Atelier also concedes "que l'aspect économique du fonctionnement des BC est en général très mal connu et étudié," that "[á] quelques exceptions prés, il n'existe pas d'analyse à posteriori des données de gestion des programs des BC, qui permettrait d'apprécier . . . leur capacité d'auto-développement, ou simplement du survie," and that it is "également frappant de constater l'absence d'analyse à priori au plan économique, du rôle, de la justification et de l'insertion dans les mécanismes de marché des BC" (11, 36).

GTZ, after an elaborate analysis of socioeconomic surveys in CB programs in Burkina Faso and Mali in 1993–94, established sine qua nons for sustainable CB operation in the Sahel zone. These also apply to most other regions with CB programs. These conditions include 50% (minimum) oscillation of the seasonal market price, 80% minimum average utilization of storage capacity, 4% maximum disappearances of stored grain (shrinkage, spoilage, theft, etc.), customary operating costs, and 93% minimum repayment rate on store releases to members on credit terms.[134] Most, if not all, of these conditions are far beyond what CBs have achieved in the 20-year history of the model. Hence, substantial subsidies will remain indispensable for their continued operation.

---

134. IFAD note on informal seminar; Günther and Mück 1995, chapter 5.

Subsidization: A Way Out?

Why attempt to institutionalize this artificial model at great cost in an economic-policy environment committed to market rule uncorrupted by the presence of privileged or subsidized players?

Three different approaches to this question are apparent in the documents quoted. (1) Subsidization is negative. The CB model may therefore be discarded and replaced by institutional devices more appropriate for national food-security and aid-distribution systems (Berg and Kent 1991). (2) Subsidization is principally negative. Under favorable circumstances some CBs could become sustainable in the medium-to-long run. Transitional subsidization ("subvention raisonnable de départ") is therefore justifiable in view of their important local, autonomous, food-security function. They should not be involved in decentralized national food-security and aid-distribution systems, except in emergencies, nor should they be franchise agents for national grain boards (FAO et al. 1992). (3) Subsidization cannot be condemned categorically. Since CBs cannot exist without subsidies, the cost of alternative food-security support (farm storage, grain boards) may need to be weighed against the cost of CB subsidization. Principally, however, CBs are not a suitable instrument for decentralized food-security stock management; for this, appropriate carrier systems will have to be developed (Günther and Mück 1995, 34).

There are powerful arguments against CB subsidization and the overconfidence in CB institutional viability in social or logistic functions (Berg and Kent 1991). (1) CBs are artificial: "CBs are not authentic grassroots institutions. When subsidies are absent, villagers do not set up these types of collective marketing organizations" (74). (2) They are unsustainable: "Under certain circumstances, subsidies can be justified. The CB track record, however, indicates that subsidization is creating institutions that are unsustainable in the medium to long term" (76) "because the cereal bank incentive structure is flawed" (5). (3) They are counterproductive: "If villagers are to organize cooperatively, success is more likely if they organize around activities that are properly the domain of collective action and not of individual entrepreneurship or management. Targets for collective activity need to be carefully selected. They should have characteristics that clearly justify joint action—in terms of scale, externalities, public goods characteristics. To choose wrongly, to go down the wrong institutional path in village organization, has numerous (negative) consequences" (63). (4) They are impractical: "CBs can play some food security role—providing free food to those who cannot afford to buy food during crisis situations . . . Outside donors would regularly be required to recapitalize such banks, but this presents the problem of moral hazard by encouraging the CB to give away the food in non-crisis situations. On the other hand, if crises are to be declared and giveaways are to be authorized by outside agents, CBs lose their appeal as independent, self-managed institutions, and a new government bureaucratic layer becomes necessary for information gathering, coordination, and control" (75–76).

From the Atelier viewpoint, CB food-security and social functions are desirable, provided economic viability is achievable in the medium term (FAO et al. 1992). The strong influence of the Berg and Kent position on the Atelier is recognizable, especially when considering that the FAO Evaluation still supported subsidized CBs for interannual (food-security/price-stabilization) storage as a substitute for the shrinking role of the Offices Céréalières (FAO 1990, 5). The Atelier's determination to see viable CBs as autonomous economic—that is, at least self-supporting—activities, including the assumption of local food security and other social roles[135] (e.g., credit provision to destitute members), is truly heroic: "si la fonction première des BC est, comme il y a quinze ans, la sécurité alimentaire, la Banque doit mettre en œuvre cette fonction en se développant comme une petite entreprise gérée de manière autonome dans un univers de plus en plus concurrentiel" (25).

The negative consequences of continued subsidization were nevertheless clearly recognized by the Atelier (27): corrupt motivation: "risque que l'adoption du projet de banque par la population se fasse plus en fonction de l'intérêt immédiat de la subvention que sur la base d'une prise en charge sur le long terme d'une activité collective de sécurité alimentaire"; jeopardy of autonomous development potential: "risque d'encourager une gestion plus laxiste de la banque (notamment en ce qui concerne le prix d'achat et de vente de céréales par la banque), qui entrave les capacités d'auto-développement et de survie"; and market distortion: "risque d'introduire des distorsions dans le fonctionnement du marché, au préjudice du commerce privé, qui reste de façon générale à encourager."

The GTZ analysis was two-sided. On one hand, it presented the CB model as economically unsustainable and unsuitable in principle for decentralized food-security management schemes (Günther and Mück 1995, 34). On the other hand, it seemed to foster the prospect that large-scale subsidization of vague concepts of CB networks provide microenterprise solutions to the food-security challenge. An internal position paper in early 1994[136] was still cool about the subject. Referring to a political tendency in Burkina Faso and Mali to regard CBs as enterprises with subsidized grain-marketing and food-security responsibilities, the paper points to the problematic management and control of such role mixing and the likely inability of governments to cope with the indeterminate financial requirements (1). Shortly after, at an informal interagency meeting in June 1994, GTZ seemed to sympathize with an expanded, public- and donor-financed role of CBs in decentralized food-security management: "the general objective of cereal banks which is food security is contradictory with the economic objective of the profitability of this exercise . . .

---

135. "La banque appartient aux villageois, elle se destine aux besoins de ses adhérants et à ce titre on ne peut exclure qu'elle puisse jouer un rôle à caractère social" (FAO et al. 1992, 25).

136. "Positionspapier 2 zu Getreidebanken-Entwurf," GTZ Projekt für Nacherntefragen, Hamburg, May 1994.

[CB subsidization might entail a] trade-off between the national [food security] budget and the decentralized budget of the cereal banks . . . [and] considerable positive trade-offs in trying to create sustainable decentralized systems which are more flexible than centralized systems."[137] These considerations were met with reservation by other participants, who questioned "how food security could be promoted in a sustainable way if on the micro level it is not financially attractive" and whether "subsidies" required "to keep micro mechanisms like cereal banks going . . . would be the policy of many countries" (6).

The position taken by Günther and Mück (1995) is ambiguous. On one hand, it reveals weaknesses nurtured by subsidization (12). On the other hand, their involved answer to the question of subsidized maintenance of CB operations needs interpretation. Subsidized CBs are contemplated as an alternative to the other (public, commercial, and individual) food-security facilities. But though the question of rural food security is given high priority, especially in its bearing on the rural exodus problem, the paper eventually dismisses the reliance on CBs in national reserve systems on account of their thinly spread, dispersed locations (34–35).

The Bamako Workshop (1996)

The Bamako workshop, an attempt by GTZ to gather representatives of donor organizations, technical agencies, and NGOs for an open discussion of the validity of the CB concept, demonstrated several features symptomatic of the tenacity of a development paradigm. Intended to center on rural marketing and food-security policy in an economic environment of market liberalization and structural adjustment, the workshop was programmed by the GTZ Projet de Protection des Stocks et des Récoltes, Hamburg.[138] This project was terminated just as preparations for the workshop started, largely as a consequence of the dwindling appeal of "post-harvest food loss reduction programs." In line with this termination, the contract of the person primarily responsible for the organization of the workshop was not renewed. She participated in the workshop itself on a part-time basis, on loan from her new posting. Workshop organization was entrusted to a consultant, a trained biologist. A Benin agricultural educationalist participated in the management of the workshop.

Attracting donor organizations, research institutions, and independent consultants did not get enough attention to secure the participation of economists and policymakers. Hence the workshop was dominated by NGO and government staff employed in CB programs that provided careers and income for most of them. Most participants were not acquainted with the principal evalua-

---

137. IFAD, note on informal seminar, 5–6, intervention by GTZ director, subdepartment for agriculture, forestry, and emergency operations.

138. A GTZ activity outsourced partly to keep headquarters staff inputs within the prescribed maximum percentage of total operational commitments.

tion reports of recent years, such as FAO et al. 1992, Berg and Kent 1991, and Günther and Mück 1995.

With apparently only a minority of attendees trained in economics or business administration, economic considerations tended to fall on deaf ears during discussions, particularly because these considerations questioned the justification for continued subsidization. Instead, a plea for heavy CB subsidization on the grounds that loss-making CBs fulfilled a (wishfully imagined) social-redistribution function met with sympathetic support.

At the ad hoc request of two participants from multilateral agencies, a small, extracurricular working group was established, in which donor and economic viewpoints were not minority views.

The workshop report mirrored the diverging recommendations of the working groups and the concluding plenary discussions: "deux idées diamétralement opposées étaient développées par les participants. D'un côté, se lisait la forte tendance de façon systématique [à éviter] l'échec des [BC] et de l'autre une évidence de cet échec."[139]

The very brief workshop "conclusions" were realistically insubstantial, regretting the missed opportunity for a constructive debate and "la durée très limitée des travaux surtout sur un sujet aussi délicat" (4). Nevertheless, in order to deliver a minimum of concrete recommendations, a "Communiqué Final" was added to the report as annex 5. These recommendations present an attempt to reach some compromises. The principal conciliation offered to the subventionists was the qualified acknowledgment of a need for support of "les projets de dépots alimentaires[140] en zone structurellement déficitaire," but a "traitement cas par cas pour la création des banques de céréales dans les autres zones, avec la volonté explicite de ne pas pérenniser le soutien mais au contraire de parvenir à un autofinancement des [BC]" (2).

A weak outcome indeed, compared to the express "objective" of clarifying "si les [BC] . . . dont faible utilisation des capacités, comptabilité incomplète, malversations et pertes considerables furent bientôt à l'ordre du jour . . . sont par essence condamnés à l'échec en raison de problèmes précis"![141]

The principal conclusion emerging from the Bamako workshop is the fundamental difference between the CB promoters (mostly NGOs) and structural-adjustment supporters (economic and financial analysts, free-market functionalists) in their respective interpretations of failure ("échec") and their attitudes toward subsidization. For the promoters, "échec d'une BC" exists when, in spite of all the (subsidized) support received, it becomes inoperative. For the

139. "Rapport de l'Atelier de réflexion sur les (BC), Bamako 27–29 Fevrier 1996" (monitor and rapporteur: Soulé Manigui), draft, GTZ/CILSS March 1996, 4.

140. The use of this term indicates the helplessness of the CB promotors faced with the unsuitability of the CB model, above all for food-security management (for a discussion of this dilemma see section 2.2.3).

141. Telefax workshop invitation, GTZ-Eschborn, 9 November 1995, 3, "objectives."

economists, it means chronic inability to break even. Subsidies are justified in the eyes of the promoters because they are indispensable for the survival of the CB model (in their view an essential element in rural development); funding of these subsidies, mostly external for the time being, is taken for granted. For the economists, subsidies are to be eliminated and avoided in principle, as they are unaffordable for LDCs and counterproductively nurture inefficiency.

The inconclusive debate on CB subsidization indicates that, whatever conceptual alternatives arise, as long as food-aid stocks need outlets and NGOs are eager to establish and nurse rural interventionist schemes, the CBs lobby will find free-rider opportunities for continued (at least nominal) existence.[142] As shown in the past, endless debates are nowhere as effective as the hard truth of no more aid money.

Fondations Nationales des Banques de Céréales?

NGOs and pseudo-NGOs (or "quangos," quasi NGOs, such as the ILO-affiliated Appui cooperative de développement assistée par le Program Alimentaire Mondial en zone Soudano-Sahelien [ACOPAM]) invented a new raison d'être for CBs, that is, to provide a political lobby for small-farmer and villager interests at regional and national levels, necessitating their amalgamation in national CB unions. By 1998, at least one such union had been reported (in Senegal), and others were being promoted, for example in Niger. Who will provide continued financial support for the supervision and subsidization of this political agglomeration of bankrupt units? Can they constitute an effective lobby when simultaneously begging their governments for subsidies?

ILO, probably the most political of the UN specialized agencies, has been one of the staunchest supporters of CB-promoting activity. In an informal interview in Geneva in 1996, however, it was hinted that the ILO had also begun to regard the CB model as a passing institution, as it had lost its alleged temporary function of filling a gap in rural marketing after state trading activities collapsed, now that private-entrepreneurial rural trade structures had revived.[143] In line with this philosophy, as well as with the apparent phasing-out of Norwegian funding of the ILO-ACOPAM program, ACOPAM announced its withdrawal from direct CB support as of September 1997.[144]

---

142. It is gratifying to note, however, that the latest (and probably last) workshop on CBs, conducted by the Catholic Relief Service (CRS; "Cereal Banks: Why Do They Rarely Work and What Are the Alternatives?" Dakar, January 1998), was courageously self-critical. After four days of discussions and field visits, the conclusions were just short of recommendations to suspend CB-establishment programs, cancel material and financial CB subsidization, and phase out organizational and management support. This outcome is all the more significant considering that CRS is a major distribution agent for U.S. food aid, a driving force behind many CB creations in the past.

143. Discussion with author at ILO headquarters, October 1996.

144. L. Dubois (consultant), "The ACOPAM Withdrawal/Transfer from Its National Field Projects (NFPs)," ILO, Geneva, September 1997, summary.

FAO's most recent contribution to the analysis of the CB dilemma, with special accent on food security, sustainability, and the role of NGOs, is being processed for publication (see Reusse 2002).

Chapter 3

Analysis and Discussion

3.1   The Paradigm Life Cycle

> Considerable time and money are wasted when we become
> blinded by the beauty of a conceptual model and lose our
> bearings, mistaking it for reality itself. We end up seducing
> ourselves.
>
> M. Chapin

Kuhn's definition (1962, 23–24) of a science paradigm is also a useful explanation of a development paradigm: "an accepted model or pattern . . . largely a
promise of success" in the "attempt to force nature into the preformed and
relatively inflexible box that the paradigm supplies." A German sociological
dictionary defines paradigm as "a pretheoretical model . . . often in anticipa-
tion of a reality that does not yet exist."[1]

Is it due to faulty paradigms that once famous development theories have
failed to produce convincing diagnostic and therapeutic approaches to the
alleged underdevelopment syndrome? Is the idea of development as a process
from basically rural to industrial society ("the great transition," Boulding
1964, 104) in itself a mighty Eurocentric paradigm under whose umbrella the
various subparadigms seek to indicate causes and remedies for "delays" in this
process?

Economies of scale, Western technology, Keynesian fiscal and monetary
policies, state-supported cooperative enterprises, and government responsibility for social and food security are all examples of paradigmatic concepts that
dominated the design of "development" models at one time or other. Intervention based on those models caused distortions with negative social, political,
and environmental effects. The growing awareness that Western industrial
civilization might be a secular[2] phenomenon may generate a more empathic
understanding of different cultures and their social organization.

The paradigm underlying the two case studies described in chapter 2 is the
prototype construct of powerless peasants lacking appropriate storage facilities
and therefore forced to dispose of most of their crops to shrewd merchants at
unreasonably low prices—possibly having to buy back the same for their daily
needs later in the season on usurious credit terms. The case studies provide
sufficient material to disprove the paradigm. As a rule, small farmers are not

---

1. "Vor-theoretisches Modell . . . häufig Vorgriff auf eine nicht vorhandene, aber für die Zu-
kunft gewünschte Wirklichkeit" (Hillmann 1994, 648).

2. In the sense of "occurring once in an age or century."

obviously powerless; that is, they normally determine the time and quantity of their crop sales in a competitive rural trading environment, disposing of alternative barter goods to mobilize cash (see p. 61). Their storage structures are low-cost, easily replicable from environmental sources, and efficient. Their storage technology is appropriate under the given environmental and economic conditions. Their sense of food security centers on reserve stocks held by the nucleus and extended family, supplemented by traditions of mutual assistance and sharing (see pp. 58–59).

The paradigm, once employed under specific historical conditions in the early European cooperative movements, failed to develop viable cooperation in most Third World countries, especially in Africa. When economic and institutional failure reduced the appeal of cooperative programs to donors, the CB model was sold as an alleged socioeconomic innovation. In fact, however, it offered but a vaguely defined precooperative activity, without the selection criteria, legal status, and commitments regulating cooperative activities, though with an even higher claim to external assistance.

The "war on waste" was based on the same paradigm, but dealt principally with its storage-technology element. In a number of countries it operated alongside the CB program, and in others it created para-CB institutions, such as the Tanzanian "village stores," in an effort to achieve economies of scale as a precondition for the effective application of "modern" storage methods.

Being conceptually weak, both programs emphasized awareness campaigns. Difficulty in convincing the affected population of the existence of a problem was interpreted as confirmation of the peasantry's ignorance.[3]

When, in the implementation of PFL, the baseline assessment efforts failed to confirm the generalized assumptions of the paradigm, these efforts were abandoned in favor of "rapid appraisal." Effectively, this meant subjective assessments aimed at identifying priority areas for improvement, in relative terms, that is, without empirical verification of the problem. This cleared the way for the implementation of a multitude of projects loyally following the original conceptual model (see pp. 34–35).

When, contrary to the promised panacea of CBs, the allegedly excessive trade profits failed to materialize and not even operational costs were recovered, other justifications were prioritized, such as "collective action" and "food security"—as though the CBs were a public service deserving financial and organizational support. It is amazing how long it took the donor commu-

---

3. Pretty and Chambers (1993, 49) refer to the "common pattern" in the "history of agricultural policy": "Technical prescriptions are derived from controlled and uniform conditions, supported by limited cases of success, and then applied widely with little or no regard for diverse local conditions. Differences in receiving environments and livelihoods then often make the technologies unworkable and unacceptable. When they are rejected locally, policies shift to seeking success through the manipulation of social, economic and ecological environments . . . This leaves decision makers cocooned in a 'self-defined' world where they blame the low rates of service utilization upon farmers' apparent apathy and 'conservatism.' "

nity to realize that CBs are, in general, not processes of collective action and do not generate local food reserves, and how tenaciously the NGOs involved tried to maintain this nimbus (see pp. 76–79).

When the expected successes failed to materialize, that is, project objectives in measurable terms were not achieved, all possible reasons were considered except failure of the concept's basic paradigm. Projects were extended and programs were expanded, although there was no proof of their viability. The response to failure was to increase inputs, enlarge the scope, replicate in different environments, create arguments for subsidization, and, above all, divert attention to new horizons (see pp. 38–39).

This tenacity in ignoring defeat, apart from being facilitated by the lack of transparency and the leniency of the aid administration, also indicates the ideological traits of a development paradigm.

One feature of this stereotypical attempt to take refuge in defiance is the legacy of unfinished elements (including an impact analysis of the implemented innovations) left to a follow-up project. Overambitious itself, this fails to critically evaluate the previous output, because of its own implementation problems. More follow-up projects stand in line to add to the number of never fully evaluated, poorly monitored, and ailing "grassroots" operations. As long as the paradigm finds believers, these operations may fall into dormancy but do not die completely. Every now and again, an agency (NGO or other) will attract donor funding for a revival or "revitalization" program, including a new series of CBs, and hopes to find another sponsor after the initial funding runs out.[4]

Thus, the institutions created under the spell of a faulty but powerful paradigm develop their own dynamic and, if necessary for survival, the art of metamorphosis.

Once it had become indisputable that the "war on waste" lacked substance, the program substituted a "systems approach" to identify improvement potential in the postharvest or so-called production-to-consumption process. But this was primarily a window-dressing maneuver with a promise of reorientation. Because no critical evaluation was made of the 15 years (200 projects) of program activities under the food-loss-reduction theme to mark the change of emphasis, the ongoing and "pipeline" projects were unaffected. Even new project requests, proposals, and documents were formulated using the old, exaggerated food-loss estimates and promises as though nothing had been learned (see p. 40).

When its core motive, that is, the replacement of the grain trader by collective storage and marketing, proved ineffective, the CB movement turned to

---

4. Jiggins, Reijntjes, and Lightfoot (1996, 100), with reference to the Sasakawa Global 2000 Program: "a familiar cycle of initial enthusiasm, followed by attempts to secure scale effects, followed by frustration and retreat, will be encountered once again, at the expense of much energy and soul searching."

and magnified secondary motives that had an attractive face value to donors. The food-security motive appeared to be most promising, a wheel of generous fund-generating capacity in the aid machine. The fact that farmers do not trust collective food security and succeed in holding interannual reserves in their traditional family stores, and that therefore CBs have no food-security function other than (at most) that of an occasional storage and distribution facility for external food-aid supplies, can only be understood by those genuinely acquainted with the environments in question.

This acquaintance is still a rare commodity in the jet-set world of "development" planners and implementers. Paradigmatic preconceptions "have too often been brought to the field in the minds of experts and extensionists together with their travel bags, and often they disappear with them at the end of a project without leaving behind a sustainable trace except some 'concrete' "[5] (Reusse 1995, 9).

When does the life cycle of a faulty but superficially appealing interventionist paradigm end? Apparently not until the aid flow supporting it stops. And even then, the paradigm might only be in suspended animation until a new generation of inexperienced enthusiasts picks it up again, probably under a new label.

3.2   Behavioral Background

3.2.1   Organizations

> Like biological populations, organizational populations acquire dynamic properties affecting their development.
>
> C. Shanks, H. K. Jacobson, and J. H. Kaplan

Development organizations live off the aid-generating power of the development (or underdevelopment) paradigm and its sub- and satellite paradigms, especially those reinforcing their specific mandate or raison d'être. For example, the paradigmatic thesis that one-sixth of humanity suffers from chronic hunger or malnutrition is the basis of mandates of several humanitarian and development organizations and NGOs to fight these two evils. It provides them with a conspicuous goal that the public can comprehend, adherence to a theme or themes derived from this goal, and the pole around which the organizational nimbus can be cultivated: the nimbus of efficient, informed, professional, and humanitarian handling of their important mandates.

The development paradigm, therefore, is the most protected area in the development organization's metabolism. Every other area may be subjected to scrutiny and internal troubleshooting, but the development/underdevelopment paradigm and its satellite paradigms carrying the organization's mandate are largely taboo. To a large extent this protection extends to the themes of special

---

5. "Concrete" refers to the critical statement by a national project director (see pp. 70–71 n. 127).

programs of action derived from those paradigms (e.g., the effective shielding of PFL against basic critique from internal evaluation; see p. 45).

This paradigm loyalty is reinforced by the paradigm's value in the market for donor funds. The most dynamic organization will dismiss a paradigm just before its market value declines, which, once started, tends to accelerate. In doing so, it will replace the old with a new paradigm. The longer such paradigm change is delayed, the less credibility is granted the organization's pledge to the new paradigm (e.g., PFL's late attempt to shift to a systems approach; see p. 42). The World Bank has demonstrated good paradigm marketing over the past two decades. Others have shown rather unimaginative and risk-averse paradigm adherence and, as a consequence, lost the intellectual lead to more dynamic institutions, even in their areas of comparative specialization (Reusse 1993, 466–67).[6]

Organizational behavior is not necessarily a top-down implementation of directives emanating from authoritative positions under strict rules and regulations, comparable to the Prussian-German civil service depicted in Max Weber's "hierarchic model" of "modern bureaucracy." Instead development organizations, especially those outside the development-financing sector, should be compared with the professional model developed since the midcentury: the organization provides the arena in which parties (professional/intellectual/ political and career networks) try to control the goals. The professional element dominates, however, because professionals are indispensable for day-to-day running of the organization.

Whether this dominance of professionalism is altogether a good feature of development organizations cannot easily be answered. The results of nearly four development decades and the ever-growing number of institutions, committees, meetings, documents, acronyms, and terms in the development sector have inspired doubts about the cost-effectiveness of all these activities and a suspicion that many are an end in themselves (in other words, l'art pour l'art) rather than a means toward realistic goals. Some sociologists see a danger that professionalism will develop its own momentum toward becoming a "futurist robot" in the service of irrational "system goals," "having spun out of control . . . until some part breaks down and the technical wonder disappears" (Quarles van Ufford 1988, 94). The perpetual sequence of projects almost ad absurdum, as observed in the case studies (see pp. 39, 68), would seem to indicate such a process.

Robust development organizations (or relevant departments thereof) are well described as arenas, in which different "constructions of reality"[7] interact.

---

6. A paradigm presently undergoing critical analysis that may lead to its slipping from its stereotypically claimed "first priority" rank is the "direct attack on poverty" as development instrument (cf., e.g., Wolff 2000). Its use as an open invitation for "any type of intervention" is being realized (see, e.g., Naudet 2000, 218).

7. Quarles van Ufford (1988, 21), drawing on Crozier.

With rare exceptions, these constructions tend to accommodate the political climate and official goals, which are necessarily those that appeal to the Western public and its governments, that is, 80% of the donor community, and in that sense may be termed ethnocentric. For example, the heavy emphasis on women's liberation and the alleviation of poverty are the product of a (hitherto) highly patriarchal and achievement-oriented cultural history. These concerns are not as important in Third World societies, despite lip-service statements at international conferences.

The main credibility problem facing all development organizations is their lack of accountability, largely determined by the difficulty of defining and measuring the targeted and untargeted results, that is, the net benefits derived from their activities. This difficulty touches on the importance of evaluation, the long and conveniently neglected management responsibility in the development machinery. With project outputs so far detached from the donor-country taxpayer's control[8] and so opportunistically or passively watched by the Third World population and their overtaxed and frequently bypassed governments, almost anything goes (see, e.g., DANIDA 1991, 42). Camouflage, face-saving, suppression of critique, calls for increased inputs and scale, and other means of refusing to admit failure protect wrong interventions for years, until management decides to take consequential action or donors become aware of the real situation and drop their support.

Unlike the conventional bilateral and multilateral development organizations, the mushrooming NGO sector is dominated by ideological, political, rent-seeking elements rather than professionals. This sector attracted comparatively lively donor interest, especially in the popular field of "grassroots"/"people's participation" development, under the impression of relatively youthful and altruistic motivations prevailing among NGO cadres at the beginning of their careers. Donor funds, always in search of outlets requiring a minimum of follow-up control, were amply available to the larger OECD country-based NGOs, which, in turn, instigated a mushrooming of local Third World NGOs as implementing agencies, motivated not least by the opportunity of taking their share of the funding bonanza.[9]

As a result, "NGDOs' [nongovernmental development organizations'] development thinking, policies and practices (became) standardized along official lines" (Wallace, Crowther, and Sheffard 1998, quoted by Fowler 2000, 641). "Southern NGOs tended to emulate their northern 'partners' and often be more intimately linked to the aid system than to the wider society" (Fowler 2000, 640).

---

8. "IOs [international organizations] do not conscript or tax individuals . . . Their dues come from nations, rather than individuals; their laws do not affect individuals directly; and there is no authoritarian appropriation of human capital and resource. Quite simply, there are fewer reasons for individuals to be angry with IOs" (Gallarotti 1991, 186).

9. Thus, more than 200 southern NGOs were born in Panama practically "overnight" after the creation of a World Bank–supported national Social Fund (VENRO 2000, 8).

While a certain amount of youthful drive and preparedness for voluntary service may still be assumed in many NGOs, there is a clear trend toward bureaucratic structures, rising overhead costs, and self-serving interests (cf., e.g., Hanisch and Wegner 1994; Bierschenk and Elwert 1993, 17). Nor can it be assumed that their political ambitions, facilitated by their position as interlocutors of aid programs, are only benevolent.[10] Their "participation in political movements" and "paternalistic approaches"[11] in a Latin American context led to the program analyst's advice to "keep an eye on NGOs' ability to stand back when it comes to identifying, planning, and executing microprojects" (Hatzius 1996, 24). VENRO (2000, 6) voices a double warning against uncritical NGO support, in view of its misuse in programs expanded beyond the management and control capacity of the participating agencies, or as alternative avenues of political and professional elites to extract rents from the international aid regime.[12]

The lack of professional expertise, especially in the field of economic analysis and evaluation, tends to be responsible for the tenacity of NGO-supported paradigmatic intervention concepts of problematic justification, such as the Sahelian CB programs. Much of the NGO boom is based on the grassroots development approach fashioned during the third development decade. These organizations seem to find it difficult to part from the "myth of self-contained . . . well integrated 'communities,' "[13] that is, "false images of communality" legitimizing "the efforts to entice the local people themselves to *do* something . . . if only they would come to 'understand' their situation"[14] and from the " 'naiveté' of organizing community action through hierarchical administrative structures" (Quarles van Ufford 1988, 31). An example of the latter is the promotion of subsidized apex (union) structures to rescue nonviable local CB creations such as "les futures unions régionales" (see p. 71)

---

10. "Participation is endowed with very diverse meanings by interlocutors who try to help, enlighten or manipulate social groups" (Stiefel and Wolfe 1994, quoted from a book review by Villarreal [1995, 796]). See p. 78 for the promotion of subsidized CB hierarchies as political lobby structures.

11. Also in Africa, reservations about what an African conference participation called "philanthropic imperialism" have grown: "you give us the help which you think we need, but you do not give us the help which we want" (van der Velden 1996, 410, 417).

12. In a salient sociopolitical analysis of the "civil society" mantra in the context of African reality, Chabal and Daloz (1999, 24) observe that "African politicians cynically exploit the image of Africa as a helpless and miserable continent in order to prompt the involvement of NGOs, from which funding and assistance are expected . . . the role of NGOs could well lead to the hijacking of genuinely needed development aid by the same old and well established elites." The authors conclude that "the present profusion of uncoordinated NGO involvement in Africa is unlikely to lead to sustained development," while being "much more eminently favourable to the instrumentalization of disorder than to the emergence of a western-style civil society."

13. Not to say that these do not exist, but that they are rare; as a rule, "communities" are divided into several clans or ethnic or religious groups.

14. Compare Harry Turay's analysis of the Sierra Leone situation (see p. 65).

and the Fondation Nationale des Banques de Céréales in Senegal (see p. 78), faithfully following the example of the failed cooperative movements of the second development decade. However, as amply apparent from African cooperatives' history, "supra-local organizations not only created a false image of village communality but also, through their mode of operation, proceeded to undermine that very image" (ibid.).

The rise of NGOs certainly has been accompanied by overconfidence in their abilities. From trust in the state as carrier of the development impulse, the development euphoria switched over to the NGO panacea (Mossmann 1994, 187–88). The ease of attracting funds promotes complacency. The "new managerialism of NGOs" shares with other aid administrations "a lack of humility, a key note of the development power/knowledge complex" (Nederveen-Pieterse 2000, 182).

Cost-effectiveness, efficiency, and impact are rarely subjects of analysis in NGO country program studies (van Dijk 1994, 36). Compare the shattering summary released by the Atelier regarding the transparency of the (largely NGO-run) Sahelian CB programs (see pp. 72–73), as well as Günther and Mück 1995 on CB feasibility studies. "So, instead of state welfare, we could be entering into the era of NGO welfare," concluded an analyst of an early trend toward using NGOs as implementing agencies in World Bank social-sector lending (de Souza 1992, 113), a trend that meanwhile has reached alarming proportions.[15] The claim for subsidization of (primarily) NGO-promoted CB creations, with moderate support from GTZ, tolerating pseudo-economic arguments in defense of wasteful if not corrupt performance and advocating their employment in decentralized national food-security schemes would seem to parallel such a trend (see pp. 75–76).

Why this inflation of NGO creations, patronized by bilateral and international aid fund-channel operators? Since aid flows existed before most, if not all (at least "southern"), NGOs were born, the latter may be seen as products of the aid business. Although many NGOs initially advocated anti-aid philosophies, today practically all are aid-integrated. Most "northern" NGOs have become "development" administrators and most "southern" NGOs implementation agents, facilitating the unconstrained flow of aid in the face of the limited absorptive capacity of public institutions in most Third World countries. Direct aid-fund support to the NGO sector is seen as constructive ("institution building") by a development policy primarily concerned with the effective implementation of development programs with conventional development targets. This impatient bypassing of public institutions in order to satisfy the self-propelling ambitions of the aid machine reflects the loss (or sclerosis) of

---

15. Eberlei 2000 provides an account of the hasty, top-down approach to employing NGOs ("the civil society") to draw up the poverty-reduction strategy papers recently requested by the World Bank as facilitator of new loan disbursements to indebted LDCs.

the capacity to question the raison d'être of aid.[16] As Fowler (2000, 638) dryly remarks: "The current system appears to be clinging to a demonstrably inadequate development model and institutional arrangements to make it happen."

Now that the self-referential egocentricity of the aid business has been questioned, the current NGO positivism needs to be critically analyzed and evaluated.[17] Research in East and Central Africa, Southeast Asia, and elsewhere revealed that the middle classes[18] had usurped NGO leadership and fund-channeling positions (Neubert 1994, 211), not infrequently motivated by personal enrichment and clientelism. The growth of a rentier mentality in the NGO business, which opts for perpetuation if not eternalization of their self-help projects' dependence on aid, goes without saying.[19] Hence it is necessary to warn against (1) the risk of extinguishing a genuine propensity toward self-help based on autonomous strength and sacrifice; and (2) the potentially negative consequences of ill-considered interventions in Third World social structures in the blind ambition to satisfy fashionable concepts of temporary aid policy.[20]

3.2.2   Donor Governments

Donor priorities generally lean toward alignment with UN-proclaimed paradigmatic development goals and with the political climate in their constituencies,[21] notwithstanding lobbying by domestic suppliers.[22] In specific fields, special (often personalized) relations with technical-assistance organizations

16. "This inward orientation causes sclerosis of perspective. Development policy becomes self-referential, oriented toward self-established targets and evaluated under self-established criteria" (author's translation from German; Neubert 1994, 194).

17. IFAD 1996 may be regarded as an early pioneer in this regard: "The desire to include NGOs in the project should be tempered by a careful evaluation of the benefits to be derived and the thorough assessment of the NGOs' capacities and relevant experience" (21). The report also warns against the fashionable substitution of NGO for government structures (allegedly weak, missing, or uncooperative), pointing at the "difference" in "permanency and sustainability; long term survival of NGOs [depending] on external grants with a limited time frame, whereas government agencies are generally more permanent" (25). This explains governments' hesitancy to accept continuing responsibility for aid-supported institutional innovations of doubtful sustainability (see, e.g., p. 70).

18. "The middle metropolitan class" (Johnson 1990, 86).

19. Cf. Hanisch und Wegner 1994, 12–13, 132–33, and Thiéba's 1992 comment on the "associations ex nihilo" (see p. 65).

20. "Especially in the funding of NGOs we must be aware of its influence on sociopolitical processes whose quality and direction we as yet hardly understand" (author's translation from German; Neubert 1994, 211); cf. also Long and Long 1992, 14, referring to the "euphoria of new populist strategies for empowering people" in the late 1980s.

21. Thus the upsurge of aid flows in the first two development decades has partly been interpreted as a "projection abroad of the [then popular] welfare state ethics" (Noël and Thérien 1995, 551).

22. Which applies to many equipment- or commodity-intensive aid programs, such as the Italian-funded PFL projects (see p. 46).

and/or NGOs play their part.[23] Intergovernmental rivalry (also via NGO activities) sometimes plays a role, for example, in the frequent duplication of efforts, with confusing effects at local implementation level (see pp. 54, 57, 59, 64).

Paradigm changes would appear to be easier at the donor level, since here funding in the short-to-medium term is largely autonomous. However, a lack of competent staff with adequate field experience, policy inertia, and political opportunism often prevent bilateral development cooperation from spearheading the abandonment of outmoded development concepts. But this does not appear to prevent subscription to newly marketed buzzword paradigms (including more recent examples such as participation, decentralization, civil society),[24] as though some ritual reorientation urge pervaded the development administration, a "ten-years' itch" as one policy analyst put it.

Given the lack of viable project concepts, fund-channel pressure has been a chronic problem in past development decades, inviting the unchecked expansion of vaguely evaluated and monitored NGO- and other donor-funded programs (see pp. 59, 68, 76)[25] and neglect of tripartite control functions in international trust-fund projects (see pp. 44, 48, 69; DANIDA 1991, 51).

More recently, budget constraints, increased competition among implementing agencies, and domestic public opinion have urged some donor governments to scrutinize their development-assistance policies and controls.[26]

3.2.3   Receiver Governments

Receiver governments' motivations in requesting or accepting aid are multifarious and often not transparent.[27] Short-term political motivations, often mixed with vested interests of persons or groups,[28] can promote aid programs with questionable or even counterproductive effects. Deliberate "passivity," as well as dramatization, may be employed to generate or maintain an aid stream (Naudet 2000, 222). Especially in the aid-funds-absorbing arena, fungibility often obscures the who and how of the final beneficiaries.

Budget and balance-of-payment support is an overriding motivation among LDCs with chronic financial problems. Quite commonly, aid projects are regarded as an opportune source of supplementary revenue (e.g., via local sale of

---

23. See p. 33 for the Dutch influence in PFL.

24. "We must examine the increasingly vocal argument . . . in favour of the putative role of civil society . . . vague and idealized as their view may be . . . The current assumption about the emergence of such a recognizable civil society in Africa is eminently misleading and derives more from wishful thinking or ideological bias" (Chabal and Daloz 1999, 17, 18).

25. Lancaster (1999, 110, 112, 113) highlights this chronic malaise in her analysis of USAID's country program performances.

26. Cf. Brüne 1995 for an account of trends in France's aid policies in Africa.

27. Wallis (1989) distinguishes between "overt" and "covert" motives of governments (quoted from Mawhood 1990, 615).

28. In particular affecting the location of aid interventions (most likely involved in situations such as those described on pp. 59, 64).

food and commodity aid supplies), as government payroll support (e.g., via the partial integration of government functions and related staff into aid projects), or as access to otherwise unaffordable benefits (e.g., the generous funding provisions for Land Rovers, electronic accessories, travel allowances, salary emoluments, overseas degree courses, etc., often a sine qua non for project permission). Such motivations partly explain the low commitment of receiver governments to preparatory, implementation, and follow-up obligations, as well as the ease with which the aid lobby markets poorly designed projects and unsuitable aid programs (see, e.g., pp. 67–68). Other motivations include creation of director/codirector positions for political supporters, employment generation for the growing number of university graduates and local consulting firms, balancing of genuine food and input supply gaps, and access to technical information and training.

Half-hearted commitment and slow delivery of counterpart contributions to development projects and the often passive, even obstructive, attitude to aid interventions are not necessarily an indication of incapacity, inertia, corrupt motives, or unawareness of existing problems. They may also be a consequence of the overtaxing of governments with aid projects and programs, and the related administrative burden of mission visits, briefings, consultations, and personal and material counterpart services;[29] the leniency of donors and implementing agencies about shortfalls in government counterpart commitments, coupled with government awareness of the fund-channel pressure; and low confidence in the aid intervention's feasibility and the abilities and motivations of the agency staff and experts (consultants), often based on locals' better knowledge of the natural and socioeconomic environment. Third World civil servants tend to hold back their personal commitment, knowledge of local reality, and judgment. Their potential contribution can be invaluable for the researcher and development activist prepared to put aside their preconceptions and to listen.[30]

Projects generate rents of one sort or other for government cadres, just as for most other parties involved. Once used to those rents, receivers opt to maintain their source—one of the main reasons why governments rarely request the termination of nonviable projects. Occasionally, however, and with increasing frequency, the desire for intellectual truth, cultural pride, and a cleaner image of Third World ethics motivates Third World counterparts and consultants to voice open criticism (see pp. 65–66, 70).

3.2.4   Target Groups

Target groups in human and natural resources development programs are predominantly populations with very limited disposable resources. Mostly they

---

29. "Le réticence à créer des cellules" (see p. 70 n. 126) is a symptomatic reaction.

30. In addition, awareness of the generally very meager salary of locals compared to expatriates, and readiness on the part of the latter to share some privileges, can be helpful.

are members of rural settlements based on smallholder and pastoral activities. The frugality of their existence, largely dependent on their skills to exploit a problematic natural environment in a sustainable manner, determines major characteristics of their behavior. With regard to externally induced interventions, such as aid programs, their behavior may be described as rational, selective, cautious, risk-averse, cost/benefit conscious, suspicious of collective/ cooperative ventures and their promoters, exploitative of windfall profit/easy-rider opportunities, and diplomatic.

Diplomacy, cultural rules of hospitality (including suppression of unpleasant truths), "benefit of the doubt" mixed with speculation for a minimum of spillover, even salvaging gains for the community[31]—these are elements in target-group behavior that facilitate optimistic "expert" assessments of the socioeconomic feasibility and adoptability of an intervention. Not to speak of the many cases in which the interventionists feel so sure about their understanding of local needs that instead of consulting with the target groups they put all their efforts into "awareness-raising" campaigns.[32] Eventually, the overconfident interventionist has to succumb in the face of evasion (or resistance) from within the overrun target groups, such as the "solidarité à rebours" (see p. 63), the alienation of intended aid product utility (e.g., renting village stores to commercial users; see pp. 59, 65), conversion of CBs into de facto "one-man enterprises" ("une affaire privée"; see pp. 57, 65), or simply autonomous liquidation (see p. 65).

Rural people, especially small farmers, are generally shrewd and conversant with the limits and opportunities of their environment. To match their knowledge is much more difficult than the outsider may anticipate. The remark by a rural development analyst studying a CB program in Mali should be given some thought: "Après tous, pour le problème de la sécurité alimentaire . . . il n'y a pas de solutions évidentes, sinon on peut supposer qu'il y a déjà long-temps que les paysans les auraient découvertes [sic]" (see p. 63).

Paradigmatic development concepts tend to create imaginary target groups such as "ujamaa villages" and other "community"-oriented social-engineering ambitions, including CBs, community storage and processing centers, credit unions, and so forth—a battlefield for grassroots development idealists as well as for rent-seeking speculators. Constant visits by these promoters and other missions, many of which might be classed as "development tourism" (Chambers 1997), have created a market for mostly young, underemployed local people able to communicate with foreigners and eager to serve as interlocu-

---

31. Especially in interventions containing construction work at community level, such spillover can be hoped for, a major factor in the local acceptance of inclusion in CB/village-store projects, which may explain the mushrooming expansion of the Tanzanian Village Store Construction Project, for example (see p. 59).

32. Overconfidence was a chronic weakness of the PFL program presentation and persistance in project designs over the program's initial years, as well as in the general CB program approach.

tors, who eventually assume the role of "spokesmen" for less initiated visitors. Their ability to adapt to promoters' paradigmatic concept of local reality and to their ambitious interventionist ideas, in the expectation of playing some remunerative role, is often quite remarkable.[33]

These "spokesmen," however, are often as unreal as the "community" concept of the "grassroots" developers. With some patience, the people of substance, on whose views the final outcome of the intervention largely depends, can be discovered. They tend to be much occupied by their farming or trading activities and to stay away from meetings of doubtful practical relevance. More genuine efforts to consult these people, which should include the "traditional leaders,"[34] and less eagerness to build castles in the air with unrepresentative "spokesmen" would have helped avoid many inappropriate projects.

3.2.5   Experts

"Experts," in this context, are development workers on short-to-medium-term contracts (including "consultants") employed by development agencies for specific tasks connected predominantly with field-program and project identification, preparation, implementation, and evaluation activities. They constitute an important link in the development-assistance machine. Ideally, they ought to serve as instruments as well as antennae in the process of aided development, continually testing goals and methods in the course of application and signaling requests for adaptation, redirection, or withdrawal where those goals or methods prove inappropriate.

Unfortunately, this ideal "expert" is rarely matched in the field. Development work needs specific talents and attitudes, apart from technical and linguistic adequacy, including the courage to question established paradigms. This conjunction of qualities is rare.

Most experts (including consultants) are subject to an insecurity syndrome under the pressure of the often unrealistic expectations of their employers (or clients) as well as of governments and target-group representatives in the receiving countries. The resulting urge for conspicuous achievement is fueled by a desire for self-realization, prestige, and career advancement. Dramatization, superficiality, opportunism, a blueprint approach, and a tendency toward over-dimensioned project inputs are largely explained by these motivations in com-

---

33. "Mais la demande est forte" (see p. 68 n. 118): the ease of silencing potential doubts by this superficial statement is a typical result of such an echoing relationship.

34. They are a more visible institution in some countries (e.g., anglophone West Africa) than in others. The excellent IFAD program-evaluation report (IFAD 1996, 26), for example, concludes with regard to the need for unbiased selection of beneficiary target-group members: "Traditional leaders should be fully incorporated into the exercise . . . This approach takes full advantage of the customary social objective of providing for everyone."

bination with expansionist program management at agency headquarters level.[35]

Other behavioral features negatively influencing field-project implementation and feedback include the insulating superiority syndrome;[36] excessive greed for power expressed in self-righteousness, stubbornness, and jealousy; and corrupt motivations, for example, personal interest in staying in a particular location or in exploitation of side benefits, underlying artificial justifications for the extension of effectively redundant posts or projects. Not that there aren't seasoned field experts and consultants with sober, professional work approaches. Wherever interventionist paradigms set the tune, however, the opportunists and dramatizers tend to take the limelight, and the insecure jump on the bandwagon for shelter,[37] while sober professionals risk falling into discredit for their nonconformist views.[38]

The tendency of field staff to become sedentary—to neglect their commitment to field research, to rest on insufficiently substantiated conceptions, and, probably to prevent others from gaining threatening insights, occasionally to discourage visiting missions from establishing genuine field contacts—has been discussed (see p. 38). Where field activities are reported, their effectiveness in terms of productive field exposure may often be minimal. Lack of field commitment, camouflaged by routine cover-up reports that "all is well," also became an identified weakness in NGO operations (Sinaga 1994, 112). The amazing neglect of CB accountability (see p. 73 for the Atelier conclusion) seems to confirm this observation.[39]

---

35. This headquarters ambition placed on the shoulders of conceptually lenient consultants and experts (most crucially project managers) is addressed in a courageous consultant report on Nepal (see p. 39 n. 35). It also underlies the chronic failure to establish a basis for sound direction of successor projects in Sierra Leone (see pp. 39–40) and the blind compliance with quantitative material targets that have obviously dominated international support projects for the Tanzanian Village Store Construction Project (see p. 59).

36. Aptly characterized by Pretty and Chambers (1993, 34): "how powerfully inhibiting is the normally dominant behavior of professionals with farmers—lecturing, criticizing, advising, interrupting, 'holding the stick,' and 'wagging the finger.' The astonishing time it has taken to realize the analytical capabilities of farmers can be attributed to this almost universal tendency of outsiders."

37. "Hence it is not surprising that those theories seem to have prevailed which gave access to the largest amount of consultancy funds . . . development economists 'knew that they were largely ineffective and felt morally uncomfortable,' but that there was a 'diplomatic imperative,' which required 'tact and tongue biting' " (Kurer 1996, 663–64, quoting Toye 1991).

38. See, e.g., the reception of the returning mission without a project (see p. 105 n. 60), the resistance to the consultant's request for more baseline research (see p. 35), management's initial reaction to Greeley's study (see p. 49), Abbott's reference to the suppression of the marketing economists' critique (see p. 33 n. 20), and the fate of a critical evaluation report (see p. 45).

39. Mintzberg's characterization (1983, 386) of the "pseudo-missionary" activist comes to mind now and then: "The organization may be staffed by volunteers, but these people are drawn to it not to pursue the external mission (the organization's ostensible purpose), but rather to satisfy some personal need they have—to socialize, gain power and prestige, or whatever."

3.3   The Ills of Aid

The ills of aid, that is, its inherent trends toward misjudgment (systems of ignorance), toward waste (easy money), toward inertia (perpetuation), toward undermining of traditional values and virtues (subversion), and toward arrogance (complacency), are interrelated with the paradigm culture. Protected by a politically opportune paradigm, these ills can grow relatively uncontrolled, while by themselves they provide fertile ground for the birth and growth of superficially analyzed paradigmatic development concepts.

3.3.1   Systems of Ignorance

> There is a strange paradox to this, namely: the little understood fact that the poor can enrich us.
>
> Dioscoro L. Umali

Systematic analysis of the knowledge dilemma accompanying paradigmatic interventions in Third World societies has been promoted by anthropologists and anthropologically inclined agriculturists and development economists in the arena of development criticism since the second half of the 1980s.[40]

Criticism based on this research is predominantly directed against "the ways in which the knowledge of the peoples being developed are ignored or treated as a mere obstacle to rational progress," thereby "constituting them as 'underdeveloped' or ignorant." Such ascriptions are seen as "a long history of changing western representations of other societies," normally in an "agentive" mode, that is, "depicting a state of affairs requiring action or intervention of some kind, usually by the party doing the depiction" (Hobart 1993, 2), an analysis quite descriptive of the nature of the interventionist paradigm (section 1.1.3).

This discriminatory attitude toward indigenous knowledge may be seen as "a secular version of the process by which monotheism converted local gods into saints, spirits and demons." In this process a new "hierarchy" develops, "cognitively based in appearance, but . . . actually one of a quite different kind of power . . . evaluated according to their salaries: from the expatriate who terminates this knowledge, via their local assistants who know the language and supply them with most of their information . . . to the locals themselves who have been thinking practically about the issues for centuries, are paid

---

40. A milestone in this revolution was the organization of an interuniversity network of English, Dutch, and German anthropologists under the auspices of European Inter-University Development Opportunities Study Group, founded in 1985. Its chairmanship rotates among the departments of anthropology, ethnology, rural sociology, agriculture, and development studies of London (Hobart, Richards), Amsterdam (Quarles van Ufford), Wageningen (Long, van der Ploeg), Berlin (Elwert, Bierschenk), and Bielefeld (Lachenmann). This European initiative ran parallel to developments in American agricultural science and rural sociology (Altieri at Berkeley, et al.).

nothing and will live with the consequences of the project for generations after the others have gone home" (Vitebsky 1993, 108).

The externally introduced "expert" tends to bypass the "art de la localité" or "savoir faire paysan," which may be characterized as "a dynamic, multi-dimensional knowledge system, and highly complicated and detailed as well, essentially a craft," predominated by the "labor process," whose "manage-ment" is directed toward "improving the valorization of the local ecosystem," "a kind of knowledge that goes directly from practice to practice[, which is] not expressed in a univocal, clear language[; however,] it is precisely this vagueness or 'imprecise' character that allows for this active process of inter-pretation and change" (van der Ploeg 1993, 209, 210).[41]

"Systems of ignorance" tend to follow the "normative institutional engi-neering" or "technocratic approach," thus insufficiently "looking at and under-standing existing informal farmer and trader practices and formal administra-tive systems," a policy researcher observes in the example of a nonviable seed-multiplication project whose planners were falling back on the "conve-nient excuses for explaining failure 'in implementation,' " one of the "escape hatches of the public policy analyst" (Biggs 1983, 60).

According to an analysis of U.S. development assistance to Third World agriculture, two dimensions of knowledge tended to be systematically dis-counted in the past, "the social science perspective" and "ethnoscience or rural people's knowledge." Where social scientists had been employed, "their job had been largely devoted to overcome this cultural/ecological resistance to 'modernization.' " It remained thereby undiscovered that "farmers often achieve a richness of observation and a fitness of discrimination that only would be accessible to western scientists through a long and expensive re-search program[;] what appeared primitive and unprogressive, was complex and sophisticated" (Altieri 1989, 86–87).

German contributions analyze the narrowness of expert knowledge, its ne-glect and even avoidance of indigenous knowledge ("Abschottung der Exper-ten"), and the target population's unproductive response, that is, confusion of confidence in traditional practices ("das Gefühl der Ohnmacht") coupled with distrust in the expert formula, which together result in withdrawal ("Strategie der Verweigerung"), which the expert views as "defensive ignorance." This unfortunate process perpetuates the isolation of the "expert knowledge." Or-ganizational survival interest supports this rigidity. Even elaborate project identification and implementation procedures, such as the "Zopp" (Zielorien-tierte Projektplanung) used by GTZ, do not escape the "system of ignorance" in the definition of development goals, without questioning the underlying

---

41. Incorporating terms developed by Bourdieu (1980) and Lacroix (1981).

assumptions and priorities and taking account of earlier failures (the "clean slate" approach: "le développement n'a pas de mémoire").[42]

"Communication requires shared meaning" (Roeling 1988, 40–41), a requirement not easily fulfilled in research work with Third World rural populations who have their own localized (often metaphoric) terminology. Therefore, "the sociologist, like the physician, should have first, intimate, habitual, intuitive familiarity with things; secondly, systematic knowledge of things; and thirdly, an effective way of thinking about things" (Whyte 1984, 282). "Pursuing well-accepted methods and theories, we may be imprisoned unwillingly within a currently popular view of the world," the same author warns (261); but, pointing at the dynamics of local knowledge systems, he observes: "While most people most of the time do things in standard ways, there is enough creativity in the human species so that in any field of activity we can find people who are doing things in new and promising ways. To grasp the nature and significance of these social interventions, we must learn to understand the technical as well as the social problems they are intending to solve" (286).

The media and the aid lobby publicize images of cruelty and suffering that tend to reflect and often exaggerate exceptional situations, yet rarely ever portray the normal life led by the overwhelming majority of Third World populations. The outsider finds it difficult to imagine that this normality, irrespective of whether it is classed above or below Western-ethnocentrically determined "poverty" lines, can be lived as well as, and sometimes more happily than, the average urban industrial Western family.[43] But even many "experts" find this hard to understand and accept, arriving in the field with preconceived notions and insufficiently prepared for a serious learning process with the target population. Many ill-conceived interventions could have been avoided from the outset, if someone acquainted with life in the target world had patiently talked to the inhabitants, in their language if possible, to find out their true priorities.[44]

A large-scale, expansive project for soil and water management in Mexico, trying to implement an elaborate model derived from the study of ancient Indian cultivation practices, was propelled into replication, eagerly donor-funded, before the promoters realized it would be a total failure. They had been so enthusiastic and protective about their model as to practically avoid

---

42. Lachenmann 1991b, 12, 13, 16, 20, 23, incorporating terms developed by, among others, Elwert 1985; Chauveau 1985; and R. Athorp, "Development: Styles of Knowledge and Ignorance," paper presented at European Inter-University Development Opportunities Study Group meeting, London, December, 1986. See also Bierschenk, Elwert, and Kohnert 1993, 17–20, with particular reference to the incapacity to learn from past mistakes.

43. "Confronted with daily horror stories of Third World human castastrophes, who of us would believe that most people in the allegedly poor countries lead a normal working and social life, far from feeling miserable or exploited" (author's translation from German; Bliss 1985, 11).

44. Cf. Bliss's analysis (ibid.) of a totally abortive German agricultural mechanization project at Farafra oasis, Egypt.

consultation with the local population: "This situation might have been avoided if representatives from the various participating agencies had simply listened to the villagers, discovered their needs, and given them an opportunity to participate in the decisions and action being taken . . . it is probably safe to say that the lack of local interest from the outset meant the project would never have worked, least of all as a 'community' endeavour" (Chapin 1988, 15).

The prevalence of a dichotomy between local and imported knowledge and the tendency of development programs to grow into "systems of ignorance," as portrayed in the anthropological discussion above, appear to broadly categorize the two cases discussed in this book: the dramatization of biased research reports and the bold promises derived therefrom (see pp. 30–33); the infantilization of local populations with respect to their postharvest technological and socioeconomic coping systems (p. 34); the excessive confidence placed in "communal" management and enterprise models (pp. 34, 53–55) developed in industrial societies (which usually failed even there); the ardent defense of these "systems of ignorance" by their operators over many years, even after better knowledge had become available (p. 60); and the nonchalant use of obsolete paradigmatic assumptions in the design and proposal of new projects and the construction of claims for their subsidization (pp. 40, 76–79).

3.3.2   Easy Money

At the root of the easy-money disease are the lump-sum aid-budget commitments of donor countries, which match public sentiment nursed by the aid lobby, and the wish to maintain or improve one's reputation on the UN stage.

Unlike the profitability criterion of private investment, the principal criterion in the investment of public development funds is their timely and even disbursement over the budget period.[45] Overestimating productive absorptive capacities at the implementation level, the UN recommendations for international and national aid-budget commitments (though honored only in part by major donor countries) led to chronic fund-channeling pressure, inviting opportunism, window dressing, and exploitation by eligible users and irresponsible inflation of project loans by development-financing institutions.[46]

An ample allocation is the primary concern of agencies, including NGOs, in this "chaotic market place of aid flows" (Quarles van Ufford 1988, 27), which results in unrealistic country programs promoted by competing agencies (cf. DANIDA 1991, 41–48). "The definitions of goals" ("ethnocentric in the sense that they appeal to western public and governments") "do not change primarily

---

45. "I want this money into Africa; the money doesn't do any good if it sits in accounts, I can assure you" (World Bank vice president Jaycox [1994, 4–5], referring to a U.S.$14 billion backlog in general lending allocation for the African region).

46. Jaycox's impatient appeal confirms the reference by Carlsson, Köhlin, and Ekbom (1994, 177) to "the pressure to lend in the World Bank," whose loan appraisal system (according to the authors) "is subordinated to the individual interests of program officers (getting projects to the Board) as well as the organization's own objectives (meeting the disbursement targets)."

because of new insights, a learning process, but because of successful penetrations into the arenas which determine access to funding" (Quarles van Ufford 1988, 20). Aid "intervention," last but not least, means "big business, not only for firms and consultancy bureaux but also for the government agencies or NGOs involved . . . [,] a commodity with a calculable exchange value that reproduces and legitimizes particular intervention practices and interests" (Long and van der Ploeg 1989, 235).

In this "greedy competition for 'relevant' projects," the discrepancy between expediently presented plans "made primarily to solve the problem of gaining access to funding" and the "actual issues surfacing in the 'implementation' " becomes symptomatic, "official designs" being characterized as "too rigid, often too grandiose and costly, leading to their demise once inflow of funding stopped" (Quarles van Ufford 1988, 26).[47] Furthermore, the progressing " 'Balkanization' of Third World countries by the aid organizations limits the capacity of national recipient bodies to generate comprehensive policies as well as sustainable institution building" (27).

The most expedient safety valve for fund-channel pressure in rural-development programs are agricultural credit schemes, typically involving the distribution of soft loans to innumerable smallholder households via expediently established collective agents at village or district level (e.g., "associations villageoises," "cereal banks," etc.). Superimposition of these schemes on a rural population principally averse to formal indebtedness has turned most of them into quasi household subsidies consumed via low and dwindling repayment rates. The conclusion of an analysis of a popular aid-funds magnet, "income-generating measures," underscores this point:

> The main responsibility for this state of affairs lies undoubtedly with many donors, who are over-eager to shower the target groups with loans without properly considering the conditions and underlying criteria involved. In addition to this there are also psychological aspects: the poorest of the poor have difficulty understanding why the "rich" donor organizations insist on the small sums involved being paid back. As a result they refuse to pay, on the (usually correct) assumption that, if it came to the crunch, nobody would be able to "get anything out of them" in any case, and another donor would be prepared to supply more credit . . . At best the result is a temporary increase in income which is not based on genuine value-added but rather, ultimately, on consumption of the loans and subsidies awarded to them. (Fischer 1996, 6, 8)

An analysis of the performance of farmers' organizations as credit agents in Senegal highlights the counterproductive effects of such easygoing utilization

---

47. Referring to Réal P. Lavergne's discussion of Canadian development aid in the same collection of essays.

of aid funds (Lachenmann 1991a, 85). The formal indebtedness and low repayment morale imported into the associated communities through the quasi-
imposed and subsequently collapsed schemes led to the desperate situation that
traditional informal credit access through rural produce traders (disqualified as
"usuraires" by the project's "animateurs") was jeopardized by the ill-guided
intervention ("les commerçants n'ont plus de confiance dans les paysans"),
leaving the population without any credit source—an example underscoring
the erratic consequences of a development cooperation "increasingly determined in ignorance about what goes on once funding decisions are taken"
(Quarles van Ufford 1988, 27).[48]

Both cases, the CBs and the war on waste, are by their very existence symptoms of the easy-money disease. As stated in Berg and Kent's excellent 1991
analysis (see p. 72): "The availability of these [aid-funded] subsidies and the
encouragement by donors and governments that they reflect explain the existence of cereal banks . . . [which] are not authentic grassroots institutions.
When subsidies are absent, villagers do not set up these types of collective
marketing organizations" (74). How this easy money attracts corrupt practices
is well described in Thiéba's observations (1992) on the French-funded "associations ex nihilo" (Senegal, see p. 65). Its general boost to petty embezzlement is suggested in Belloncle's experience (Mali, see p. 62).

The constant push for expansion of the PFL program once funds had been
secured and the resulting unending sequence of inconclusive projects;[49] the
chronic neglect of socioeconomic feasibility; the wasteful inflation and "balkanization" of the aid scene through hasty intervention programs leading to
faulty location and duplication;[50] the overkill in food-aid supplies and its counterproductive effects (see p. 61)—all these are symptoms of the same disease:
easy money.

In the end, the outcome of such overfed programs is almost predisposed to
the negative, as the Berg and Kent verdict on the CB movement confirms:
"Because of the magnitude of the resources that have been devoted to creating
and nurturing CBs, these results have to be regarded as nothing less than disastrous" (Berg and Kent 1991, 52). Langerbein (2000, 26), referring to sub-
Saharan Africa in general, simply states: "There was too much aid which often
suffocated possibilities of self-help . . . [while giving] the power elite access to
considerable sinecures."

---

48. FAO and more recently GTZ have shifted emphasis on savings, pointing to the need for
"safeguarding savings deposits" in rural areas, while scrutinizing the focus in lending operations
on "repayment or the debt capacity of the borrower" (Mittendorf and Kropp 1990).

49. "Receding horizons," see pp. 38–40.

50. See, e.g., Niger (see p. 64), Tanzania (see p. 59), and Laos (see p. 54). Cf. Brett 1993 for
Uganda.

3.3.3   Perpetuation

The predominance of securing continued access to aid funds and the comparative neglect of thorough identification, evaluation, and control of goals and
interventions within funded programs favors the perpetuation of ineffective
and even counterproductive development activities. "As a matter of fact, the
organizational need for control is not great, as long as the top is able to con-
vince its sponsors that policy is well implemented, or that more funds are
needed because of grave development problems . . . It is only when the 'political climate' of the context which controls inflow of funding changes that a
reconstruction of official goals is considered" (Quarles van Ufford 1988, 22).
Thus, while the funds keep flowing into the ongoing projects and programs
without substantial reorientation at the implementation level, "policy making
(at agency level) is a continuous process in which goals are reconstructed as
the money flow reaches new configurations, actors and interests" (ibid.).[51]

The lip-service flexibility at agencies' fund-securing top does not affect the
rigidity of their "pipeline" implementation.[52] At this level, failure has to become conspicuously obvious before a comfortable outlet for secured funds will
be abandoned or curtailed.[53]

> "Failure" is seldom a reason (at best it is one of the pretexts) to halt a
> particular intervention policy. Normally "failures" are the starting point
> for the elaboration of the next round of interventions,[54] one could even
> argue that a certain degree of "failure" is strategic in the reproduction of
> intervention itself.[55] . . . [Policymakers often are] not looking for the best
> way or most efficient alternative to solving a problem. They are instead
> searching for support for action already taken, and for the support that
> serves the interests of various components of the policy-shaping com-
> munity. (Long and van der Ploeg 1989, 243, quoting Palumbo and
> Nachmias 1983)

To go a step further, the importance of "the capacity to control definitions
of what is supposed to be happening locally is of the utmost importance to the
agencies and, in a way, they constitute their . . . 'logo' in the development

---

51. Examples are the search for political justification for the perpetuation of CB subsidization
by GTZ and ACOPAM and—at least for a temporary raison d'être vis-à-vis the inescapable
consequences of the universal liberalization/structural adjustment drive—by ILO (see pp. 74–79).

52. Cf. FAO director general's SOFA 1982 statement, in contrast to PFL program management routine, p. 37 n. 30.

53. "In the absence of crisis there will be little reconsideration of past choices, subject to what
Peter Blau terms the elasticity of demand for advice" (P. M. Haas 1997, 34).

54. Cf. the replacement of loss-assessment baseline studies by "rapid appraisal" (pp. 34–35).

55. Examples are the numerous projects to revive the milling industry in Sierra Leone (see pp.
39–40) and the innumerable NGO projects for the "revitalization" of CBs in the Sahel.

market . . . In other words, the images of the local scene must be made to fit organizational needs" (Quarles van Ufford 1993, 140). In this example, "reporting at the local level was 'managed.' The intermediate levels made sure that the continuity of their existence was secured. And indeed, for some good reason, their superiors did not wish officially to 'know better' themselves" (141). The conclusion is plausible: "The survival of development policy and its administration are dependent on sufficient ignorance . . . it greatly encourages to ignore facts about the local level . . . this construction of both knowledge and ignorance provides some sort of stability" (142).

A strong anchor of this stability is the mentality of the middle-level development administrators and professionals: the administrator protecting continuity of routine performances; the professional tending to settle for personal views of reality acquired in formative, but not necessarily significant or recent, training and/or experience, which he or she often feels disinclined to change.[56] And, as aptly described by an analyst, "institutionally, it is very hard . . . to alter drastically existing programs and policies, even if the intellectual support for these programs might be waning. What planners typically do is to alter programs in such ways that new components are fitted to old programs . . . it also retains a sense of bureaucratic familiarity with programs, which is essential for mustering institutional support for the new components" (Sanyal 1994, 25).

To summarize, an analysis of the two case studies shows that the following causal elements are responsible for the perpetuation of intervention programs developed on wrong or outdated paradigms:

- Uncritical acceptance of paradigmatic assumptions (see pp. 28, 30–34, 53–54, 58)
- Replication of interventions before their validity in the field was established (see pp. 38–40, 59, 67–68)
- Neglect of field research (see pp. 34–35, 45, 58) and of monitoring and evaluation of field reports
- Gaps in keeping up with the state of the art (see pp. 33–34, 37–38, 49, 59–60)
- Insufficient attention to critical voices and evaluation advice (see pp. 35, 45, 72)
- Failure to identify, admit, and learn from conceptual mistakes (see pp. 34, 47–48, 66, 71, 77–78)
- Paradigm protection through focusing on problems of implementation ("escape hatches"; see pp. 36, 95)
- Refuge in defiance (see pp. 38–39, 67–68, 78–79)

---

56. "Such categorical thinking facilitates regular work routine, at the risk, however, of crowding out unbiased factual observation and innovative initiative" (author's translation from German; Marx 1972, 9).

- Evasion of evaluation, economic, and financial accountability (see pp. 54, 60–61, 71)
- Weak execution of monitoring commitments (including face-saving motivations) (see pp. 44–45, 48, 68–69)
- Repetition of outdated "project objective" and "background" components in the presentation of new project proposals (see pp. 39–40, 66–68)
- Unsatisfactory donor performance in screening proposals for viability (see pp. 57, 61, 64–66)
- Face-changing mechanisms to please donor preferences (see pp. 42, 55, 76–79, 81–82)
- Political/ideological support, including food-aid-distribution interests (see pp. 30–32, 51–57, 60–62, 66, 70–71, 78–79)
- Policy, program, and pipeline inertia (see pp. 34, 39–40, 61, 68)

3.3.4 Subversion

Development engineers like to make a clean sweep of things, that is, they concentrate on what in their opinion is lacking and largely negate or belittle existing assets. They rarely ask what helped the societies in question to survive in a usually frugal, if not hostile, natural environment. Hence, they fail to recognize a number of vital existing assets, especially those of human and social capital.[57] These include local skills and experience, especially in the sustainable exploitation of their natural habitat; personal and collective strategies of endurance and adaptation to periods of stress; mutual assistance, task force, and the management of communal resources; exchange networks supported by often far-flung "spades of trust"; and traditional ethics, often superior to those imported from "developed" societies.

"Development" intervention without due knowledge of and respect for those assets may at best fail, and at worst subvert local value systems, and thereby act against sustainable development. "Past lessons indicate that both receiving NGOs as well as donor agencies must keep in mind that how aid is channelled can make the difference in either strengthening or debilitating civil society" (Aldaba 2000, 273).

Debilitating interventions in this sense tend to erode

- *The carrying capacity of the habitat* through destructive land clearing, cultivation, and large-scale irrigation systems under ill-conceived subsidy schemes.
- *Productive and constructively entrepreneurial energy* through excessive maintenance of adolescents in formal educational processes and the sub-

---

57. For examples of spectacular cases of substitution of human and social capital for financial capital in the creation of wealth in "backward" societies, see Reusse (1973, 1982) on Ghana's cocoa and Somalia's nomadic livestock industry.

sequent (largely futile) search for white-collar jobs, preferably urban-based; inflation of aid-dependent government and public institutional structures (including subsidized cooperatives) and their staffing (see pp. 43, 59, 64, 70, 76–79); extensive lobbyism and speculative suspension of self-help action in expectation of aid (see pp. 60–64, 66, 77–79); and dilution of the objective and subjective value of money, fueled by a disproportionate and/or inappropriate injection of aid, inviting greed for rapid personal enrichment via patronage, corruption, or exploitation, and frustrating the less privileged (see pp. 56–57, 60–66).

- *Cost-consciousness, thrift, and sustainability principles,* through aid-supported subsidization and budget support, as well as capital-intensive, import-intensive, or otherwise wasteful aid projects (see pp. 54, 56, 59, 61–63, 78).

- Communal *resource management systems,* through the introduction of Western (individualized) land rights for the facilitation of formal agricultural credit schemes (see pp. 14–15).

- *Organically grown mutual assistance and task-force systems,* through the importation of ideologically inflated and subsidized cooperative (and paracooperative) movements, with heavy financial and technical external assistance (see pp. 15, 55–57, 60–61, 65–66).

- *Traditional exchange, trust, and credit networks,* through subsidized public and cooperative trading and banking activities, largely based on aid support (see pp. 62–65, 98–99).

- *Local skills, knowledge, and technologies,* through their relative subjective devaluation against aid-supported introduced ("modern") technologies of allegedly higher productivity (see pp. 14, 35, 47).

- *Coping and survival strategies,* through reliance on food and emergency aid (see pp. 15, 60–61).

- *Local production and marketing systems,* through the disincentive effects of ill-managed food and commodity aid (allocation, timing, and distributive arrangements) (see pp. 60–61); and the subsidized attempts to replace the rural produce trader by public or communal marketing ventures (CB) (see pp. 51–52, 55, 57, 70, 72).

- Government *authority, responsibility, and accountability,* through direct aid interventions via NGOs, premature loyalty shift to the "civil society bandwagon" (the "flavor of the month," van Rooy 2000, 306),[58] or creation or expansion of unsustainable governmental or parastatal units and their staffing under aid-supported salary scales (see pp. 54, 57, 59–61, 64–66, 71).

---

58. "It would be highly premature for development studies to replace the paradigmatic importance of the state by that of civil society" (Schuurman 2000, 19). "The dichotomy between state and civil society . . . taken for granted in most current interpretations of African politics, does not reflect realities on the continent" (Chabal and Daloz 1999, 17). See also relevant footnotes on pp. 86, 89.

- The *human resource of potentially useful local and expatriate development workers at field and agency level,* through their being locked into unproductive programs and projects of low learning potential (see pp. 39–40, 43).
- Confidence *in international cooperation,* through the disillusioning, counterproductive, and subversive effects of ill-conceived projects and their "development ruins" (see pp. 43–44, 48, 70–71, 78–79).

3.3.5   Complacency

Lords of Poverty (Hancock 1989) and *Politics of Poverty* (Abbott 1992), titles of essays critical of development politics, reflect the authors' strong reaction to the pervading complacency in professional and management decisions in organizations that claim to know how to put "backward" nations on the path of development. The discrepancy between the rhetoric of jet-set travelers on issues of poverty and malnutrition and their lavish allowances has been amply publicized. It is only human to become complacent when one has the power to direct a flow of money of quasi-anonymous origin into uses of almost equally anonymous benefit. All the more so when long-distance management makes it conveniently difficult to satisfy rarely voiced requests for qualitative accountability.

In the course of the third development decade, the overconfidence of the "development" activists started to dwindle, in many cases turning into frustration, an almost equally unproductive extreme as long as it does not lead to decisive reorientation. What remains is often a composition of self-confident façade, discreet admission of frustration, and pragmatic muddling through for organizational self-preservation and personal job (or career) continuity. Complacency does not admit total failure. Instead, a "ritual listing of excuses for 'failure' helps to propagate [an] unproductive approach" (Biggs 1983, 62), harbored by an "organizational culture" that "discourages hard-nosed analysis, unpleasant decisions, and the termination of any task once started."[59]

The only means to end the stagnant state of complacency is comprehensive, that is, quantitative and qualitative, accountability, supplemented by an objective, third-party evaluation that includes intervention goals and policies and a postintervention impact study. The latter "would also look at the consequences of interventions on other, more 'autonomous' modes of development" (Long and van der Ploeg 1989, 237).

As it is, however, "the rules of the game called 'evaluation' are conditioned more by the social interests of those involved in manufacturing, promoting, selling and utilizing this particular commodity than by the functions it is assumed to fulfill in the intervention model" (235). Rarely do "evaluations ques-

---

59. Andrew Macmillan, principal adviser, Investment Center Division, FAO, in discussion with the author, September 1998.

tion the whole idea of planned intervention and the rationality of planning"; they rather come "to play a useful role in confirming the self-fulfilling prophecy that interventionist policies are indeed viable and ideologically sound" (236). There is still a whiff of blasphemy about fundamental criticism, even if only negating the need for a high-flying intervention program,[60] since "intervention aims to bring the dynamics of local initiative in line with the interests and perspectives of public authorities and to reproduce the image of the state (or substituting agency) as being the key to development" (ibid.).

It may therefore be appropriate to keep in mind the warning from an international development conference that identified the lack of accountability mechanisms as the principal root of complacency in the development bureaucracy: "Not the views of those who are affected by policy but of those who ensure an inflow of development funds are decisive for the organization's continuity over time. Accountability thus implies great organizational interests. If unchecked it will directly serve specific needs for the organization's survival" (Quarles van Ufford 1988, 34).

3.4   Interactions/Interdependencies around the Interventionist Paradigm

A network of mutually supportive interactions comprises the interventionist paradigm in the different phases of its life, the behavioral pattern of principal actors, and the causality of propensities plaguing the aid world (the "ills of aid"). These interactions are presented in the diagram below; the arrows indicate the give and take relationships. Thus, the birth of a paradigm, for example, is favored by the eagerness of "experts" for recognition, the organizations' striving for raisons d'être and project funds, the fragmentary or distorted image of Third World reality (systems of ignorance, which the paradigm tends to re-create), and the fund-channel pressure to find convincing themes (easy money).

The two elements in support of the paradigm through all four phases of its life cycle, that is, systems of ignorance (lack of shared knowledge; see section 3.3.1) and easy money (inappropriate control over the allocation, use, and effectiveness of aid), are the major causes of wasteful (and eventually harmful) paradigmatic interventions. Next in importance are the power ambitions of organizations and experts, followed by various motivations of governments and target groups (partly created through subversive effects of paradigmatic aid-fund allocation), and the inherent trend of aid programs to become perpetual.

---

60. The sudden fright of the young agricultural engineer at a divisional task-force meeting on his return from a PFL project identification mission in 1983, upon seeing the stunned reactions around him when he reported "no major need for intervention" in the Burmese milling industry, may symbolize the situation (personal communication with staff member concerned, September 1995).

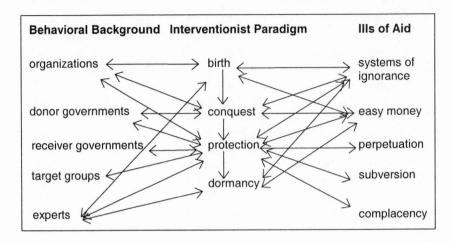

This supportive environment becomes particularly effective in the paradigm's protection phase, that is, when it clings to its role in spite of new and better information. In this phase, all ten relevant agents of influence contribute to reinforce its tenacity.

By placing the paradigm in the center of the interaction web and attending to the support it receives from its environment, it is possible to overlook how it supports this environment. The support, however, is strong in both directions, which brings up a chicken-and-egg question: Are interventionist paradigms at the root of the increasingly unconvincing profile of the aid business, or is it the latter that generates and nurses these paradigms? Both viewpoints appear plausible. If the whole Western post–Second World War "development" initiative is understood as the product of one grand interventionist paradigm (see sections 3.1, 3.2.1), however, the conundrum of the chicken and the egg would appear answerable.

Independent of this answer is the realization of an orchestra of interrelations, interactions, and interdependencies in the aid-generating, -channeling, and -implementing process, favoring the birth and longevity of superficially conceived interventionist paradigms. This realization should suggest corrective measures for various components, most effectively for the crucial ones: systems of ignorance, easy money, and perpetuation/complacency.[61]

---

61. Including the propensity to copy fashionable models, float with the tide, "do like the others" (François Mazaud in discussion with the author, November 1998); see section 1.1.5 for analysis of this behavioral trait among international organizations.

Chapter 4

Conclusions and Recommendations

This study confirms the initial hypothesis that unrealistic interventionist para-digms, that is, misguided concepts of Third World realities that provoke a need for intervention, are at the base of inappropriate development policies. It also illuminates the auxiliary role of specific systemic trends, such as the lon-gevity of systems of ignorance; the ease of access to, and lack of accountabil-ity for, funds; the propensity to perpetuate, replicate, and copy projects and programs, regardless of obvious problems; the neglected analysis of counter-productive effects (e.g., corruption, subversion of local culture); the compla-cent role of fund-channeling authorities in generating, supporting, and protect-ing such paradigms; and the accommodation of these trends in certain behavioral propensities. Any effort to resolve this problematic situation, which resembles a vicious circle, needs to realize the present constellation of main actors in the development arena.

The widening of the gray area in the classification of countries and regions as developed or underdeveloped threatens the fragile solidarity of the tradi-tional donor community. National security, private investment, and trading interests increasingly assume a leading role in influencing the dimensions and directions of aid flows, followed by disaster response and private benevolent "development" sponsorship, while the importance of conventional ODA con-tinues to decline. The threat of privatization turns national development-assistance agencies into quasi-consulting enterprises intent on justifying their existence by satisfying their clients, that is, the parties paying the bill,[1] rather than serving the objective interests of the receiving country. NGOs continue to lobby for public funds and strive to expand their operations and staff, turning a blind eye to criteria of sustainability. Many UN organizations concerned with development assistance that have expanded far beyond their "regular" program (financed from membership fees) into bilaterally funded trust-fund activities find it difficult to reduce these activities in favor of higher-quality "regular" (i.e., principally normative) program performance, due to vested interests in existing operational structures. Development-financing institutions, facing reduced or even negative net loan disbursement due to massive repayment of loans approved during the expansionary second and third development de-cades, continue to promote new project and program loans under soft appraisal criteria, including debt forgiveness, in order to alleviate the embarrassment.

---

1. Cf. GTZ's internal reorientation exercise of the mid-1990s, centered on its "service" role. Similar shifts of emphasis are apparent in NRI. "Market" and "client" orientation also affects the policies of a growing number of NGOs.

Against such a background in the institutional arena, fundamental improvements toward more realistic, that is, knowledgeable, cost-effective, and sustainability-conscious, development assistance will not be easy to implement. Nevertheless, having analyzed the principal, almost chronic (or systemic), weaknesses of the "development" enterprise, and witnessing the growing disenchantment of the "man at the source," that is, taxpayers in OECD-member states, I would feel irresponsible not to provide suggestions for therapeutic measures.

In fact, basic structural and policy changes appear necessary, if development aid is to regain the confidence of the public in both donor and receiver countries. Such changes would aim to break the vicious circle by raising the level of self-responsibility, accountability, and sense of ownership at all levels from basic sponsor to target beneficiary. A careful assessment of a receiver's capacity to make best use of the assistance, as well as a substantial self-help commitment to support the authenticity of a request, would seem indispensable. There would have to be much better coordination of aid activities, best put under the responsibility of receiver governments, as well as a functional division between ODA and NGO activities. Instead of facilitating the present trend of NGOs transforming into fund-channeling agents for public institutions, their concentration on activities tailored to the funding capacity of their private sponsor constituencies appears to be the appropriate option. In the final analysis ODA, like other public-agency activities, should be subjected to privatization scrutiny.

The following recommendations take these considerations into account. They derive from a constructive search for therapeutic options of escape from the aid-pathology supporting the interventionist paradigm. As a package, these recommendations can hardly attract unanimous affirmative response, as they threaten vested interests, apart from meeting with different views from the wide arena of development policy research. Their immediate aim therefore is to challenge routine views and practices and open a debate on new avenues in defining and structuring development assistance.

4.1   Principal Restructuring Elements

4.1.1   Retrenchment, Ownership, and Self-Help Component

Supply-driven aid has led to an abundance of ill-coordinated aid activities in many receiving countries, most visibly in LDCs, jeopardizing the development of "ownership" at all recipient levels, from central government to the rural target community. A decisive turn from a supply-driven to a demand-driven aid system is overdue. For this change to take place, aid must solely be based on a recipient's "authentic" request supported by a firm and substantial self-help commitment, which must embrace the medium- and long-term servicing and maintenance provisions where required.

4.1.2   Capacity and Coordination

No aid activity should be promoted, or conducted, in receiver countries without their government's permission, coordination, and control. Before a request for assistance is granted, however, the receiver government's capacity to responsibly manage its ownership commitments must be assured.[2]

4.1.3   Private versus Official Development Assistance: Division of Roles

NGO activities, inflated by their lobby for public donor funds, have contributed much to the congestion and dramatization of the aid arena. A division of funding constituencies, activity focus, accountability, and political conditionality between ODA and NGO assistance is recommended.

Under such a scenario NGOs would depend predominantly on their private sponsors, and not only in donor countries. These sponsors harbor growth potential if prudently cultivated through more genuine information,[3] control, and participation entitlements. Even more than now, NGOs should concentrate on direct assistance at the community level.[4]

ODA, on the other hand, should downplay its paradigmatic commitment to direct poverty alleviation. Instead, it should concentrate on infrastructural improvements at the national and regional level, and on assistance in the development of higher education, research, public management, and fiscal/economic policy. Contrary to NGO assistance, ODA should be under stringent conditionality, that is, requiring receiver governments' visible adherence to structural adjustment/good governance principles. While direct poverty relief and improving quality of community life would be the paramount object of NGO assistance, ODA's primary function would be the strengthening of government capacity as administrator of the "common good."

4.1.4   Quality over Quantity

Measures suggested above would lead to a healthy contraction of aid flows. From the resulting lower level, a gradual increase should be based on qualitative criteria rather than quantitative. Secured by the firmly anchored self-help commitment, aid would correspond to priority needs felt and communicated by the receiver rather than conceived and propagated by the donor,[5] with positive effects on the sustainability of the invested improvements.

---

2. An exception is humanitarian aid, where a government has abdicated its management authority to an aid organization or international trustee.

3. Public support via provision of regular time on national TV channels for authentic reports on NGO work may be considered, allocated to individual NGOs following a schedule negotiated with a national NGO association or committee.

4. For a recent analysis of trends and opportunities in the role played by NGOs in development assistance, see Reusse 2001a.

5. See Bliss 2001 for a persuasive plea for a genuinely demand-driven aid concept.

4.2   Evaluation

In order to foster the integrity of evaluation units in technical and financial aid agencies, the creation of an international bureau of evaluation[6] should be considered. As an autonomous institution, the bureau should carry out, supervise, or review evaluations (including theme, impact, and ex post evaluations) of aid projects or programs on request; develop and promote international standards of quality and integrity of evaluation tasks in the development-assistance arena; and offer a specialized servicing facility to assist LDC governments in the appraisal of foreign investment and loan proposals, including those promoted by international development-financing institutions. Governance of this institution would require an adequate representation of the donor community, including the NGO sector and national taxpayer associations in major donor countries. It would report simultaneously to the Development Assistance Committee of OECD, the Economic and Social Council of the UN, and IMF.

4.3   UN Technical Agencies

Instead of competing with NGOs and bilateral agencies at the project level, UN agencies should concentrate on their traditional domains, that is, their normative roles in their fields of specialization. In this endeavor they should strengthen their advisory capacity to serve not only the Third World but all member governments as well as development-finance institutions, NGOs, and (on questions of considerable socioeconomic and/or environmental interest) the private sector; explore possible scenarios of relevant future concern, avoiding overdramatization, in the manner of an international think tank; promote regional and global discussion, negotiation, and consensus on questions of transnational importance; promote global transparency through gathering and dissemination of relevant and professionally vetted information and analyses; and monitor development-assistance activities, including the issue of "leading-edge" reports indicating trends and warning against misdirection of resources.

In order to raise the agencies' capacity to perform these functions, trust-fund donors should consider redirecting extrabudgetary contributions into "regular budget" support, for example, via a voluntary membership fee increase. Staff recruitment and development should be scrutinized, aiming at the highest available qualification and suitability, subjecting even senior staff positions to selection procedure and staff rotation systems,[7] eliminating "political" appointments, subordinating criteria of geographical representation to

---

6. Also conceivable as a "standing commission" made up of a team of respected individuals from various institutional backgrounds meeting periodically and supported by a small professional secretariat and its own budget (Masakatsu Kato, FAO Evaluation Service, in discussion with the author, November 1998)

7. A "healthy tidal movement of staff" (Richard Roberts, head of FAO Marketing and Credit Service, in discussion with the author, February 1999) would help import new ideas and experiences from outside, e.g., the private sector.

those of functional competence, and offering attractive employment conditions, incentive systems, and career prospects.

NGOs in need of professional information, evaluation and advice, or a forum for discussion, should meet an active support facility at the agencies, while providing the latter with the grassroots contacts vital for research and policy generation in place of the agencies' declining field programs.

4.4   Anthropological (or Reality Experience) Year

The aid bureaucracy is increasingly staffed with young career professionals with inadequate or nonexistent field experience. Such cadres cannot provide the "humus" for the generation and implementation of realistic development policies. The introduction of an anthropological (or reality experience) year, that is, a postgraduate field experience extending throughout a full crop-season cycle, spent living and working in a rural community of an LDC,[8] should therefore be a precondition for a professional career in aid agencies, including major NGOs.[9]

Through liaisons with national or regional research institutions, the incumbent would be a valuable link and spokesperson for the villagers' queries and requests, and vice versa. His or her research would include political, cultural, and economic linkages with the regional and national systems of which the community is an integral part, as well as impediments and opportunities in the community's development related to these systems.

The entrance requirements (completed academic education, supplemented by an introductory course in Third World socioeconomics and rural sociology) would ensure the incumbent's ability to use a reality-experience year productively as a life experience of singular professional relevance.

4.5   Accountability to the Basic Providers of Funds

In order to make public development transfers more transparent to the OECD-country taxpayers, and the aid-channel operators more accountable to them, a departure from the present funding system might be considered.

The present system, allocating aid funds from the national budget, fails to create a sense of ownership among the tax-paying community. This would change if taxpayers were given the freedom to opt (by declaration in their tax return) for a percentage of their pretax income to be allocated to public devel-

---

8. The country should differ ecologically or culturally from their home country for incumbents from LDC countries.

9. Finance would not be a serious problem, as the voluntary host community would be expected to provide customary accommodation. With remuneration principally limited to frugal subsistence and travel allowances and adequate insurance coverage, the reality-experience year would require more than material interest in the profession, and would thus effectively screen out opportunists and political appointees.

opment funds. These funds would thus be based on voluntary contributions.[10] This tax allocation would be accompanied by intensified rules securing transparency of public aid activities as well as the taxpayers' right to demand special evaluation and audit reports by independent consultants. The improved transparency should also enable the target beneficiaries to help identify channel distortions, leakages, and other irregularities.

Private sponsorship to NGOs should be income tax–deductible only if the benefiting organization (or program) is predominantly[11] privately funded, in order to discourage excessive lobbying for public funds by these organizations. The current lobby system detracts from productive activity and obscures lines of reporting and accountability. Public control over NGO performance should be intensified in order to raise the quality and accountability of these organizations, in the particular interest of their private sponsors, whose sense of "ownership" should be strengthened.

Enhanced taxpayer control should also help achieve a desirable upgrading of donor-country representation on governing bodies entrusted with the guidance and control of international organizations. These representatives must have the qualifications, commitment, and courage to take, maintain, and defend a critical though unpopular stance, when objectively required.[12]

4.6   Privatization of Aid?

The more direct linkage between those who give from their own resources and the beneficiaries of their donations strongly recommended in this chapter may be seen as a step toward a privatization of aid. Such privatization could mean that, apart from major infrastructure and public management support, most grant-aid transfers would eventually be privately sponsored, mostly via NGOs.

Would privatization be conceivable also for the development-finance sector, presently served by the international, regional, and bilateral development banks as well as by public credit guarantees extended to commercial lending operations? Opening this sector to the private banking system through the introduction of a "development bonus," that is, an interest-rate subsidy covering the extraordinary (mostly political) risk of a development credit, might be

---

10. A departure from the classical fiscal principle of untied revenue generation becomes conceivable if development aid is defined as an extraordinary expansion of national-revenue use beyond classical government responsibilities.

11. Present dependence of European NGO budgets on public sources has been estimated as "on average up to 69%" ("Evaluation of the EU-NGO Cofinancing Programme," 8).

12. A major reason for the continuous degradation of the system's qualitative performance is lack of courage among the principal financial contributors to the UN system in demanding independent evaluation and auditing of programs and projects, according to Hagen (1988, 56). It has to be realized, however, that at the root of the deficient donor commitment to this role lies the UN voting system (one country, one vote), which breeds resignation among donor country representatives with regard to the potential result of critical interventions.

worth considering. The risk factor would be assessed periodically for each developing country.

The management and funding of such a "development bonus" system, a responsibility probably best placed in the finance ministries of the donor countries in consultation with the Development Assistance Committee of the OECD and the IMF, could thus become the principle public role in development assistance. Just as for public grant-aid transfers, the application of the "development bonus" facility should be made conditional on the borrower countries' adherence to structural adjustment/good governance principles.

In order to forestall an irresponsible expansion of lending volumes at the risk of other lenders or the public purse, no public guarantee would be given, nor first creditor rights. This should equally apply to the present international and bilateral development-finance institutions, which also may eventually come under privatization option.

4.7   Globalization with Tact

Many societies, especially those that are poor or strongly religious, see globalization as a threat to their culture. The magnetism of Western civilization, particularly for their younger generations, is painfully felt. A voluntary restraint from an overly expansionist propagation of Western lifestyles and values should be considered, not least in remembrance of the tragic events of 11 September 2001.

Culture, which includes political systems, family structures, gender roles, and the definition of human rights, may become the last fortress of individuality for societies in a globalized economy; the last trump in competition within an increasingly standardized world system.

While no culture can be protected against the silent competition from other cultures within the prevailing and probably irreversible global environment, development policy (and aid policy in general) should exercise respect and neutrality toward local cultures. This would mean, for instance, the exclusion of cultural demands from the conditions determining eligibility for assistance. The definition of "good governance" would have to remain centered on macroeconomic, fiscal, and legal discipline, and eradication of corruption.

We would do well to recall that it hasn't been that long since the West adopted a good many of those values it now claims as the final goals of history. Less than a generation has passed since Switzerland, one of the most civilized Western nations, extended voting and other essential rights to women.

Ideally, private investment and trading strategy, too, should grasp the importance of a culture-sensitive activity profile for lasting harmonious cooperation.

4.8   "Development Aid, End It or Mend It"

An international conference debating the legitimacy, quality, and impact of development assistance should be organized. The conference would provide a forum for development critique and discussion of concepts for development cooperation within the ongoing economic, political, and cultural globalization process. A possible forum organizer might be the UN University (Tokyo) in cooperation with one or more internationally renowned aid-critical institutions.

References

Abbott, J. C. 1992. *Politics and Poverty: A Critique of the Food and Agriculture Organization of the United Nations*. London.

Aldermann, H., and G. Shively. 1991. "Prices and Markets in Ghana." Cornell Food and Nutrition Policy Program, Working Paper 10, May.

Alesina, A., and D. Dollar. 2000. "Who Gives Foreign Aid to Whom and Why?" *Journal of Economic Growth* 5, no. 1:33–64.

Altieri, M. A. L. 1989. "Rethinking the Role of U.S. Development Assistance in Third World Agriculture." *Agriculture and Human Values* 6, no. 3:85–91.

Armbrüster, M., and G. Dresrüsse. 1993. "Social and Cultural Aspects of Postharvest Systems." In *International Symposium on Grain Conservation, Drying, and Storage*, 75–92. Canela, Brazil.

Aurois, C. 1995. "The State of the Art in Development Studies and Paradigmatic Prospects." In M. Simai, ed., *The Evolving New Environment for the Development Process*, 120–41. Tokyo.

Barber, B. 1961. "Resistance by Scientists to Scientific Discovery." *Science* 134:596–602.

Barnes, B., and D. Edge, eds. 1982. *Science in Context*. Cambridge, Mass.

Bauer, P. T. 1963. *West African Trade: A Study of Competition, Oligopoly, and Monopoly in a Changing Economy*. London.

———. 1991. *Frontiers of Development: Essays in Applied Economics*. Cambridge, Mass.

———. 1993. *Development Aid: End It or Mend It*. San Francisco.

Bauer, P. T., and G. M. Meier. 1994. "Traders and Development." In G. M. Meier, ed., *From Classical Economics to Development Economics*, 135–44. Cambridge, Mass.

Behnke, R. 1994. "Natural Resource Management in Pastoral Africa." *Development Policy Review* 12:5–27.

Berg, E., and L. Kent. 1991. "The Economics of Cereal Banks in the Sahel." Prepared under contract for USAID and Development Alternatives, Inc. (DAI), Bethseda, Md., March.

Bierschenk, T., and G. Elwert. 1991. "Entwicklungshilfe und ihre Folgen: Ergebnisse empirischer Untersuchungen im ländl. Westafrika." Sozial- anthropologische Arbeitspapiere, Berlin.

Bierschenk, T., G. Elwert, and D. Kohnert. 1993. Introduction to T. Bierschenk and G. Elwert, eds., *Entwicklungshilfe und ihre Folgen*, 7–40. Frankfurt am Main.

Biggs, S. D. 1983. "Awkward but Common Themes in Agricultural Policy." In E. J. Clay and B. B. Schaffer, eds., *Room for Manoeuvre: An Exploration of Public Policy Planning in Agricultural and Rural Development,* 59–73. London.

Billetoft, J., and T. Malmdorf. 1992. "Bangladesh: Addicted to Aid: Which Way Out?" Centre for Development Research Project Paper 93.2. Copenhagen, December.

Black, J. K. 1999. *Development in Theory and Practice: Paradigms and Paradoxes.* Boulder.

Bliss, F. 1985. "Wenn die Betroffenen 'sprachlos' bleiben." *Frankfurter Allgemeine Zeitung,* 11 December, 11.

―――. 2001. "Die Entwicklungshilfe auf den Kopf stellen." *Welt-Rundschau,* 17 April.

Boulding, K. E. 1964. "Economic Development: The Difficult Take-Off," In K. E. Boulding, *The Meaning of the 20th Century,* 104–20. New York.

Bourdieu, P. 1977. *Outline of a Theory of Practice.* Cambridge.

―――. 1980. *Le Sens Pratique.* Paris.

Boxall, R. A., M. Greeley, et al. 1978. "The Prevention of Farm-Level Food Grain Storage Losses in India: A Social Cost-Benefit Analysis." Institute of Development Studies Research Reports, Brighton, Sussex.

Brett, E. A. 1993. "Voluntary Agencies as Development Organizations." *Development and Change* 24, no. 2:269–304.

Brewin, C. 1994. Book review of P. Taylor, *International Organizations in the Modern World: The Regional and Global Process. Journal of Common Market Studies* 32, no. 2:267–268.

Brüne, S. 1995. *Die französische Afrikapolitik: Hegemoniale Interessen und Entwicklungsanspruch.* Baden-Baden.

Cameron, J. 2000. "Development Economics, the New Institutional Economics, and NGOs." *Third World Quarterly* 21, no. 4:627–35.

Carlsson, J., G. Köhlin, and A. Ekbom. 1994. *The Political Economy of Evaluation: International Aid Agencies and the Effectiveness of Aid.* Basingstoke.

Chabal, P., and J. P. Daloz. 1999. *Africa Works: Disorder as Political Instrument.* Oxford.

Chambers, R. 1993. "The State and Rural Development: Ideologies and an Agenda for the 90s." In Colclough and Manor 1993, 260–78.

―――. 1997. *Whose Reality Counts? Putting the First Last.* London.

Chapin, M. 1988. "The Seduction of Models: Chinampa Agriculture in Mexico." *Grassroot Development* 12, no. 1:10–17.

Chauveau, 1985. "Mise en Valeur Coloniale et Développement." In Olivier de Sardan, ed., *Paysans, Experts, et Chercheur en Afrique Noir,* 143–66. Paris.

Choi, Y. B. 1993. *Paradigms and Conventions: Uncertaincy, Decision-Making, and Entrepreneurship.* Ann Arbor.

CILSS. 1986. "La Reforme de la Politique Céréalière dans le Sahel: Le Burkina Faso." Paris, March.

Colclough, C., and J. Manor, eds. 1993. *States or Markets: Neo-liberalism and the Development Debate.* Oxford.

Coleman, J. S. 1971. "The Development Syndrome." In L. Binder, ed., *Crises and Sequences in Political Development,* 73–101. Princeton.

Collier, P. 2000. "Economic Causes of Civil Conflict and Their Implications for Policy." Development Research Group, World Bank.

Compton, J. A. F., P. S. Tyler, P. S. Hindmarsh, P. Golob, R. A. Boxall, and C. P. Haines. 1993. "Reducing Losses in Small Farm Grain Storage in the Tropics." *Tropical Science* 33:283–318.

Corbridge, S. 1990. "Post-Marxism and Development Studies: Beyond the Impasse." *World Development* 18, no. 5:623–39.

Costello, M. J. 1994. "State Softness as a Product of Environmental Uncertainty." *Journal of Developing Areas* 28:345–64.

Coulter, J. 1994. *Liberalization of Cereal Marketing in Sub-Saharan Africa: Lessons from Experience.* NRI Marketing Series, vol. 9. Chatham Maritime, England.

Coulter, J., and P. Golob. 1991. *Tanzania: A Case Study.* Chatham Maritime, England.

———. 1992. "Cereal Marketing Liberalization in Tanzania." *Food Policy* 17 (November/December): 420–30.

Crozier, M. 1963. *Le Phénomène Bureaucratique.* Paris.

DANIDA. 1989. "Monitoring the Field-Effectiveness of Multilateral Development Agencies: Case Study of FAO in Nepal." Copenhagen.

———. 1991. *Effectiveness of Multilateral Agencies at Country Level: FAO in Kenya, Nepal, Sudan, and Thailand.* Copenhagen.

Devaradjan, S., A. S. Rajkumar, and V. Swaroop. 1999. "What Does Aid to Africa Finance?" Development Research Group, World Bank, Washington, D.C.

Dijk, M. P. van. 1994. "The Effectiveness of NGOs." In Hanisch and Wegner 1994, 27–44.

Dolidon, D. 1980. "Evaluation du Program de Banques de Céréales." FOVODES, Ouagadougou. Pages 7–8 translated into English by TPI.

Dollar, D., and W. Easterly. 1999. "Aid, Investment, and Policies in Africa." Preliminary version. Development Research Group, World Bank, Washington, D.C.

Donge, J. K. van. 1995. "Development Theory, the Problem of Order, and a History of the Longue Durée." *Journal of Development Studies* 32, no. 3:282–88.

Eberlei, W. 2000. "Taking a Lead in the Fight against Poverty?" *Development and Cooperation,* no. 3/2000: 23–24.

Ehrenreich, B. 1989. *Fear of Falling.* New York.

Elwert, G. 1985. "Die Verflechtung von Productionen." *Kölner Zeitschrift für Soziologie* Sonderheft 26:379–402.

FAO. 1990. "Evaluation des Banques de Céreales au Sahel." Rome, October.

————. 1995. "FAO Proposals for Organizational Statements on the Future Role and Function of GASGA." Paper presented at annual GASGA meeting, Eschborn, June.

FAO/Agricultural Marketing and Rural Finance Service (AGSM). 1996. "Agricultural Marketing in FAO: Concepts, Policies, and Services." Officially distributed policy brief. Rome.

FAO, CILSS, BIT, and ACOPAM. 1992. *Atelier de Réflexion sur les Banques de Céréales.* Rome and Geneva.

Finnemore, M. 1993. "International Organizations as Teachers of Norms: The United Nations Educational Scientific and Cultural Organization and Science Policy." *International Organization* 47, no. 4:565–91.

————. 1996. "Norms, Culture, and World Politics: Insights from Sociology's Institutionalism." *International Organization* 50, no. 2:325–41.

Fischer, W. E. 1996. " 'Income-Generating Measures': Development Policy Term Which Requires Explanation." *Agriculture and Rural Development Review* 3, no. 1:56–59.

Foucault, M., and G. Deleuze. 1987. "Die Intellektuellen und die Macht." In M. Foucault, *Von der Macht des Wissens.* Frankfurt am Main.

Fowler, A. 2000. "NGDOs as a Moment in History: Beyond Aid to Social Entrepreneurship or Civil Innovation?" *Third World Quarterly* 21, no. 4:637–54.

Gallarotti, G. M. 1991. "The Limits of International Organization: Systematic Failure in the Management of International Relations." *International Organization* 45, no. 2:183–220.

Geddes, B., J. Hughes, and J. Remenyi, eds. 1994. *Anthropology and Third World Development.* Geelong, Victoria, Australia.

Granato, J., R. Inglehart, and D. Leblang. 1996. "The Effect of Cultural Values on Economic Development: Theory, Hypotheses, and Some Empirical Tests." *American Journal of Political Science* 40, no. 3:607–27.

Greeley, M. 1982. "Farm-Level Post-harvest Food Losses: The Myth of the Soft Third Option." *IDS Bulletin* 13, no. 3:51–79.

————. 1990. "Post-harvest Technologies: Implications for Food Policy Analysis." EDI Analytical Case Studies no. 7. Washington, D.C.: World Bank.

Guggenheim, H. 1991. "Of Millet, Mice, and Men: Traditional and Invisible Technology Solutions to Post-harvest Losses in Mali." In D. Pimentel, ed., *World Food, Pest Losses, and the Environment,* 109–50. Symposium 13, American Association for the Advancement of Science, Washington, D.C.

Gunilla, A., and B. Beckmann. 1985. *The Wheat Trap: Bread and Underdevelopment in Nigeria.* London.

Gunn, S. 1990. "Somalia." In P. Powelson and R. Stock, *The Peasant Betrayed,* 2nd ed., 145–64. Washington, D.C.

Günther, D., and O. Mück. 1995. "Les Banques de Céréales Ont-Elles Fait Banqueroute?" Originally published as "Getreidebank bankrott?" GTZ, Eschborn, November.

Haas, M. 1992. *Policy and Society: Philosophical Underpinnings of Social Science Paradigms.* New York.

Haas, P. M. 1997. "Introduction: Epistemic Communities and International Policy Coordination." In *Knowledge, Power, and International Policy Coordination.* Columbia: University of South Carolina Press.

Hagen, T. 1988. *Wege und Irrwege der Entwicklungspolitik.* Zurich.

Hancock, G. 1989. *Lords of Poverty.* London.

Hanisch, R. 1993. "Does Foreign Aid Develop? The Lesson from Africa." *Quarterly Journal of International Agriculture* 32:114–21.

Hanisch, R., and R. Wegner, eds. 1994. *Nichtregierungsorganisationen und Entwicklung: Auf dem Weg zu mehr Realismus.* Schriften des Deutschen Übersee-Instituts Hamburg, no. 28. Hamburg.

Hannan, M. T., and J. Freeman. 1989. *Organizational Ecology.* Cambridge.

Hatzius, T. 1996. "The Institutional Dimension of Sustainability in Rural Development." Diskuss.-schriften no. 49, University of Heidelberg.

Helms, J. 1996. "Saving the U.N.: A Challenge to the Next Secretary General." *Foreign Affairs* 75, no. 5:2–7.

Hilhorst, J., and S. Sideri. 1995. "Dutch Bilateral Aid Policies in the Period 1977–1993." Institute of Social Studies Working Paper 189. The Hague, March.

Hillmann, K.-H. 1994. *Wörterbuch der Soziologie.* Stuttgart.

Hobart, M., ed. 1993. *An Anthropological Critique of Development: The Growth of Ignorance.* London.

Hopkins, R. F. 1992. "Reform in the International Food Aid Regime: The Role of Consensual Knowledge." *International Organization* 46, no. 1:225–64.

Houghton, J. 1985. "Cereals Policy Reform in the Sahel: Burkina Faso." Elliot Berg Associates for CILSS, Paris.

Huntington, S. 1979. *Political Order in Changing Societies.* New Haven.

IFAD. 1996. "Country Portfolio Evaluation (Ghana), Executive Summary." Rome, November.

Illich, I. 1992. "Needs." In W. Sachs, ed., *The Development Dictionary: A Guide to Knowledge as Power,* 88–101. London.

Jackson, T., and D. Eade. 1982. *Against the Grain: The Dilemma of Project Food Aid.* Oxford: Oxfam.

Jaeger, W. K. 1992. "The Causes of Africa's Food Crisis." *World Development* 20, no. 11:631–45.

Jaycox, E. 1994. "Capacity Building: The Missing Link in African Development." Transcript of speech delivered at World Bank Regional Conference, Accra.

Jean, F., and J. C. Rufin, eds. 1996. *L'Economie des Guerres Civiles.* Paris.

Jiggins, J., C. Reijntjes, and C. Lightfoot. 1996. "Mobilising Science and Technology to Get Agriculture Moving in Africa: A Response to Borlang and Dowswell." *Development and Policy Review* 14:89–103.

Johnson, M. 1990. "NGOs at the Crossroads in Indonesia." In Rice 1990, 77–92.

Kiely, R. 1996. Book review of D. Moore and G. Schmitz, *Debating Development Discourse. Journal of Development Studies* 32, no. 6:959–61.

Knop, E. 1995. Book review of S. J. Tisch and M. B. Wallace, *Dilemmas of Development Assistance: The What, Why, and Who of Foreign Aid. Rural Sociology* 60, no. 2:352–55.

Krueger, A. O. 1995. Review of D. H. Lumsdaine, *Moral Vision in International Politics. Economic Development and Cultural Change* 43, no. 3:671–73.

Krugman, P. 1992. "Towards a Counter-counter-revolution in Development Theory." Paper presented to the World Bank Annual Conference on Development Economics, Washington, D.C.

Kuhn, T. S. 1962. *The Structure of Scientific Revolutions.* International Encyclopedia of Unified Science, vol. 2, no. 2. Chicago.

Kurer, O. 1996. "The Political Foundations of Economic Development Policies." *Journal of Development Studies* 32, no. 5:645–68.

Lachenmann, G. 1991a. "Soziale Bewegungen als gesellschaftliche Kraft im Demokratisierungsprozess in Afrika?" *Afrika Spektrum* 26, no. 1:73–98.

———. 1991b. " 'Systems of Ignorance': Alltags-/Expertenwissen: Wissenssoziologische Aspekte im Kulturvergleich." Sozialanthropologische Arbeitspapiere des Instituts für Ethnologie der Freien Universität, no. 38. Berlin.

Lacroix, A. 1981. *Transformations du Procès de Travail Agricole: Incidences de l'Industrialisation sur les Conditions de Travail Paysannes.* Grenoble.

Lancaster, C. 1999. *Aid to Africa.* Chicago: University of Chicago Press.

Lang, F. P., and R. Ohr, eds. 1996. *Openness and Development.* Heidelberg.

Langerbein, H. 2000. "Does Aid Do Harm?" *Development and Cooperation,* no. 3/2000: 25–26.

Ledoux, G. 1987. "Proposition d'un Système d'Evaluation Quantitative des Stock Paysans et Villageois au Sahel." OECD and CILSS, Paris, September.

———. 1988. "Etude des Problèmes et Solutions Éventuelles Associées aux Excédents de la Production Céréalière Nationale (Burkina Faso)." FAO, Rome, December.

Lincoln, Y. S. 1985. *Organizational Theory and Inquiry.* Beverley Hills.

Long, N., and A. Long, eds. 1992. *Battlefield of Knowledge.* London.

Long, N., and J. D. van der Ploeg. 1989. "Demythologizing Planned Intervention: An Actor Perspective." *Sociologia Ruralis* 24, nos. 3/4:226–49.

Luhmann, N. 1984. *Theorie Sozialer Systeme.* Frankfurt.

———. 1992. *Beobachtungen der Moderne.* Opladen.

Lumsdaine, D. H. 1993. *Moral Vision in International Politics: The Foreign Aid Regime, 1949–1989.* Princeton.

Malhotra, K. 2000. "NGOs without Aid: Beyond the Global Soup Kitchen." *Third World Quarterly* 21, no. 4:655–68.

Marx, F. M. 1972. Introduction to N. Luhmann, *Funktionen und Folgen normaler Organisation,* 7–14. Berlin.

Mawhood, P. 1990. Review of M. Wallis, *Bureaucracy: Its Role in Third World Development. African Affairs* 89, no. 357:614–15.

Mayer, W. M., W. Stevenson, and S. Webster. 1985. *Limits to Bureaucratic Growth.* Berlin and New York.

Mayntz, R. 1992. "Modernisierung und die Logik von Interorganisatorischen Netzwerken." *Journal für Sozialforschung* 32, no. 1:19–28.

Mayntz, R., and R. Ziegler. 1975. "Soziologie der Organisationen." In R. König, ed., *Handbuch der empirischen Sozialforschung,* 9:444–513. Englewood Cliffs, N.J.

McMichael, P. 1996. "Globalization: Myths and Realities." *Rural Sociology* 61, no. 1:25–55.

Meyer, C. A. 1995. "Opportunism and NGOs: Entrepreneurship and Green North-South Transfer." *World Development* 23, no. 8:1277–89.

Meyer, J. W., and B. Rowan. 1977. "Institutionalized Organizations: Formal Structure as Myth and Ceremony." *American Journal of Sociology* 83:340–63.

Mintzberg, H. 1979. *The Structuring of Organizations.* Englewood Cliffs, N.J.
———. 1983. *Power in and around Organizations.* Englewood Cliffs, N.J.

Mittendorf, H. J., and E. Kropp. 1990. "Rural Financial Markets in Africa: The Challenge for Reform." In *Entwicklung und Ländlicher Raum,* no. 6. Reprinted in GTZ Sonderdruck, pp. I–VI.

Moore, D., and G. Schmitz. 1995. *Debating Development Discourse.* London.

Mossmann, P. 1994. "NRO als Stütze für Demokratie." In R. Hanisch and R. Wegner, eds., *Nichtregierungsorganisationen und Entwicklung: Auf dem Weg zu mehr Realismus,* 177–92. Hamburg.

Najam, A. 1996. "NGO Accountability: A Conceptual Framework." *Development Policy Review* 14:339–53.

Naqvi, S. N. M. 1993. *Development Economics: A New Paradigm.* New Delhi.

Narayana, E. A. 1992. "Bureaucratization of Non-governmental Organizations: An Analysis of Employees' Perceptions and Attitudes." *Administration and Development* 12, no. 2:123–38.

Naudet, J. D. 2000. "Finding Problems to Fit the Solutions. 20 Years of Aid to the Sahel." OECD/Club du Sahel, Paris.

Nederveen-Pieterse, J. 2000. "After Post-development." *Third World Quarterly* 21, no. 2:175–98.

Nett, J. C. 1994. "Kollektives Handeln in Afrika: Probleme und Perspektiven." In *Social Strategies,* 239–54. Monographs on Sociology and Social Policy, vol. 27. Basel.

Neubert, D. 1994. "Die Rolle von Nicht-Regierungsorganisationen im Prozess des politischen und gesellschaftlichen Wandels in Kenia und Ruanda." In Hanisch and Wegner 1994, 193–218.

Newitt, M. 1995. *A History of Mozambique.* London.

Niemeijer, D. 1996. "The Dynamics of African Agricultural History: Is It Time for a New Development Paradigm?" *Development and Change* 27:87–109.

Noël, A., and J.-P. Thérien. 1995. "From Domestic to International Justice: The Welfare State and Foreign Aid." *International Organization* 49, no. 3:523–53.

North, D. C. 1990. *Institutions, Institutional Change, and Economic Performance.* Cambridge.

———. 1994. Paper presented to the Conference on Public Choice Theories and Third World Experience, London School of Economics.

OECD. 1990. *A Review of Donors' Systems for Feedback from Aid Evaluation.* Paris.

———. 1995. *The Chinese Grain and Oil Seeds Sector: Major Changes Underway.* Paris: OECD.

———. 1996. *Globalization and Linkages to 2020.* Proceedings of High-Level Expert Meeting, Paris.

Okello, R. 1996. "Women, Africa to Be Targeted." *Food Summit Agender,* Rome and Nairobi, 15 November, 4.

Oxfam. 1982. Press release introducing T. Jackson and D. Eade, *Against the Grain: The Dilemma of Project Food Aid.* Oxford.

Palumbo, D. J., and D. Nachmias. 1983. "The Preconditions for Successful Evaluation: Is There an Ideal Type?" *Policy Sciences* 16, no. 1:67–80.

Pfeffer, J. 1982. *Organizations and Organization Theory.* Boston.

Please, S. 1992. "Beyond Structural Adjustment in Africa." *Development Policy Review* 10:289–301.

Ploeg, J. D. van der. 1993. "Potatoes and Knowledge." In M. Hobart, ed., *An Anthropological Critique of Development: The Growth of Ignorance,* 209–27. London.

Pottier, J. 1996. "Agricultural Rehabilitation and Food-Insecurity in Post-war Rwanda: Assessing Needs, Designing Solutions." *IDS Bulletin* 27, no. 3:56–75.

Pretty, J. N., and R. Chambers. 1993. "Towards a Learning Paradigm." New Professionalism and Institutions for Agriculture, Institute of Development Studies Discussion Paper 334. Brighton, England.

Quarles van Ufford, P. 1988. *The Hidden Crisis in Development: Development Bureaucracies.* Amsterdam.

————. 1993. "Knowledge and Ignorance in the Practices of Development Policy." In M. Hobart, ed., *An Anthropological Critique of Development: The Growth of Ignorance,* 135–60. London.

Reusse, E. 1973. "The Role of Cocoa in the Development of Socio-economic Structures in Ghana." Paper presented at Institute pour le développement économique et politique (IDEP) Seminar on the Emergence of Agrarian Capitalism South of the Sahara, Dakar.

————. 1976. "Economic and Marketing Aspects to Post-harvest Systems in Small-Farmer Economies." *FAO Bulletin of Agricultural Economics and Statistics* 25, nos. 10/11. Reprint, Rome.

————. 1982. "Somalia's Nomadic Livestock Economy: Its Response to Profitable Export Opportunity." *World Animal Review* 43:2–11.

————. 1984. "Marketing and Input Supply." Annex to Agriculture Sector Review (Ghana), World Bank Mission Report, Washington, D.C.

————. 1987. "Liberalization and Agricultural Marketing: Recent Causes and Effects in Third World Economies." *Food Policy* (November) 299–317.

————. 1993. "Quo Vadis, FAO?" *Food Policy* 4 (December): 466–70.

————. 1995. "Post-harvest Systems Analysis and Development: A Strategy for Assistance." GTZ-commissioned contribution to the annual GASGA meeting, Eschborn, June.

————. 2001a. "NGDO at the Crossroads." *Development and Cooperation,* no. 6/2001:18–20.

————. 2001b. "What Was Wrong with Structural Adjustment." *Development and Cooperation,* no. 1/2001: 23–24.

————. 2002. "Performance of Cereal Banks in the West African Sahel." FAO Agricultural Policy and Economic Development Series (English and French). Rome.

Reusse, E., et al. 1968. "Report on Maize Farm Storage and Marketing Survey, 1966/68." Ghana Food Research Institute, Accra.

Rice, R. C., ed. 1990. *Indonesian Economic Development Approaches: Approaches, Technology, Small-Scale Textiles, Urban Infrastructure and NGOs.* Clayton, Australia.

Rich, D. Z. 1994. *The Economic Theory of Growth and Development.* Westport, Conn.

Roberts, R. A. J. 1975. "The Role of Credit in Farm Development." *Finafrica Bulletin* 2, no. 2:39–65.

Roe, E. M. 1995a. "Critical Theory, Sustainable Development, and Populism." *Telos* 103, no. 1:149–62.

————. 1995b. "Except Africa: Postscript to a Special Session on Development Narratives." *World Development* 23/6, no. 2:1056–69.

Roeling, N. G. 1988. *Extension Science: Information Systems in Agricultural Development.* Cambridge.

Rooy, A. van, 2000. "Good News! You May Be out of a Job: Reflections on the Past and Future 50 Years for Northern NGOs." *Development in Practice* 10, nos. 3–4:300–318.

Rothstein, R. 1979. *Global Bargaining: UNCTAD and the Quest for a New International Economic Order.* Princeton.

Ruggie, J. G. 1975. "International Responses to Technology." *International Organization* 29, no. 2:557–84.

Ruttan, V. W. 1999. "The Transition to Agricultural Sustainability." In *Proceedings of the National Academy of Science* 96, Irvine, Calif., 5–6 December.

Ruttan, V. W., and Y. Hayami. 1984. "Toward a Theory of Induced Institutional Innovation." *Journal of Development Studies* 20, no. 4:203–23.

Sachs, W., ed. 1992. *The Development Dictionary: A Guide to Knowledge as Power.* London.

Sahn, D. E. 1994. *Adjusting to Policy Failure in African Economies.* Ithaca, N.Y.

Sanderson, S. K. 1995. *A General Theory of Historical Development.* Oxford.

Sanyal, B. 1994. "Ideas and Institutions: Why the Alternative Development Paradigm Withered Away." *Regional Development Dialogue* 15, no. 1:23–33.

Scherr, A. 1995. "Niklas Luhmann: Konturen der Theorie autopoetischer sozialer Systeme." In B. Schäfers, ed., *Soziologie in Deutschland,* 145–57. Opladen.

Schuurman, F. J. 2000. "Paradigms Lost, Paradigms Regained? Development Studies in the 21st Century." *Third World Quarterly* 21, no. 1:7–20.

Schwab, P. 1995. Book review of J. A. Widner, ed., *Economic Change and Political Liberalization in Sub-Saharan Africa. Journal of Developing Areas* 29 (July): 566–68.

Scott, W. R. 1992. *Organizations: Rational, Natural, and Open Systems.* Englewood Cliffs, N.J.

Shanks, C., H. K. Jacobson, and J. H. Kaplan. 1996. "Inertia and Change in the Constellation of International Governmental Organizations." *International Organization* 50, no. 4:593–621.

Shanmugaratnam, N., T. Vedeld, A. Mossige, and M. Bovin. 1992. "Resource Management and Pastoral Institution Building in the West African Sahel." Discussion paper 175. World Bank Africa Technical Department Series, Washington, D.C.

Shimomura, Y. 1995. Book review of J. Carlsson, G. Köhlin, and A. Ekbom, *The Political Economy of Evaluation: International Aid Agencies and the Effectiveness of Aid. Developing Economies* 33, no. 3:362–65.

Simai, M. 1996. "Globalization, Multilateral Cooperation, and Development." Working paper, Institute for World Economics, Hungarian Academy of Science, Budapest.

Sinaga, K. 1994. "Beyond the Edge: An Assessment of Internal Limitations of Indonesian NGOs." In R. Hanisch and R. Wegner, eds., *Nichtregierungsorganisationen und Entwicklung: Auf dem Weg zu mehr Realismus,* 99–118. Hamburg.

Smillie, I. 1998. "Optical and Other Illusions: Trends and Issues in Public Thinking about Development Co-operation." Paper presented at the OECD Conference on Stakeholders for Development Operation, Paris. OECD, January.

Smith, B. C. 1996. *Understanding Third World Politics: Theories of Political Change and Development.* Basingstoke.

Souza, H. de. 1992. "NGOs in the Nineties." In UNDP, ed., *Development, International Cooperation, and the NGOs: First International Meeting of the NGOs and the U.N. System Agencies,* 113–16. Rio de Janeiro.

The State of Food and Agriculture (SOFA). 1968, 1969, 1976, 1977, 1978. Annual review, FAO, Rome.

Stevens, C. 1983. Book review of T. Jackson and D. Eade, *Against the Grain: The Dilemma of Project Food Aid. IDS Bulletin* 14, no. 2:56–57.

Stiefel, M., and M. Wolfe. 1994. *A Voice for the Excluded: Popular Participation in Development.* London.

Streeten, P. P. 1995a. Book review of S. N. M. Naqvi, *Development Economics: A New Paradigm. Economic Development and Cultural Change* 44, no. 1:209–15.

———. 1995b. *Thinking about Development.* Cambridge.

Taylor, P. 1993. *International Organizations in the Modern World: The Regional and Global Process.* London.

Thérien, J. P., and C. Lloyd. 2000. "Development Assistance on the Brink." *Third World Quarterly* 21, no. 1:21–39.

Thiéba, D. 1992. "Pas de Formule Miracle (Banque de Céréales au Sénégal)." *Chronique: Réseaux Technologie, Culture et Développement* (Dakar), June, 14–16.

Tisch, S. J., and M. B. Wallace. 1994. *Dilemmas of Development Assistance: The What, Why, and Who of Foreign Aid.* Boulder.

Toye, J. 1987. *Dilemmas of Development.* Oxford.

———. 1991. Comments on Ranis's essay "The Political Economy of Development Policy Change." In G. M. Meier, ed., *Politics and Policy Making in Developing Countries: Perspectives on the New Political Economy,* 111–19. San Francisco.

Toynbee, A. J. 1961. *A Study of History.* London.

TPI. 1979. "A Practical Assessment of Food Losses Sustained during Storage by Smallholder Farmers in the Shire Valley Agric. Devel. Project Area of Malawi 1978/79." TPI publication G 154. Slough, England.

Tvedt, T. 1998. *Angels of Mercy or Development Diplomats? NGOs and Foreign Aid.* Oxford.

Tyler, P., and C. J. Bennet. 1993. *Grain Market Liberalization in Southern Africa: Opportunities of Support to Small-Scale Sector.* Chatham, England.

Tyler, P., and R. A. Boxall. 1984. "Post-harvest Loss Reduction Programs: A Decade of Activities: What Consequences?" Tropical Stored Products Information, no. 50. Slough, England.

Union of International Associations, ed. 2000–2001. *Yearbook of International Organizations.* Munich: Saur.

Vandergeest, P., and F. H. Buttel. 1988. "Marx, Weber, and Development Sociology: Beyond the Impasse." *World Development* 16, no. 6:683–95.

Velden, F. van der. 1996. "Development Cooperation in Transition." In G. Koehler et al., *Questioning Development,* 403–25. Marburg.

VENRO. 1998. "Der neue Lomé-Vertrag: Welche Rolle für die NRO?" VENRO Arbeitspapier no. 5. Bonn.

———. 2000. "Bedeutung der Zivilgesellschaft für nachhaltige Entwicklung in Entwicklungsländern." Öffentliche Anhörung des Bundestags-Ausschusses für wirtschaftliche Zusammenarbeit und Entwicklung, Stellungnahme R. Hermle, VENRO, Bonn, June.

Villarreal, M. 1995. Review of M. Stiefel and M. Wolfe, *A Voice for the Excluded. Journal of Development Studies* 31, no. 5:795–97.

Vitebsky, P. 1993. "Is Death the Same Everywhere?" In Hobart 1993, 100–115.

Walker, J. 1995. "Every Man a Sultan: Indigenous Responses to the Somalia Crises." *Telos* 103:163–72.

Wallace, T., S. Crowther, and A. Sheffard. 1998. *The Standardization of Development: Influences on U.K. NGO Policies and Procedures.* Oxford.

Wallis, M. 1989. *Bureaucracy: Its Role in Third World Development.* London.

Warner, K. 1991. *Shifting Cultivators: Local Technical Knowledge and Natural Resource Management in the Humid Tropics.* Rome.

Watts, M. 1986. "Geographers among the Peasants: Power, Politics, and Praxis." *Economic Geography* 62, no. 4:313–86.

Weber, M. 1930. *The Protestant Ethic and the Spirit of Capitalism.* English edition. Berkeley.

———. 1978. *Economy and Society.* Revised English edition. Berkeley.

Whaites, A. 1996. "Let's Get Civil Society Straight: NGOs and Political Theory." *Development in Practice* 6, no. 3:240–44.

Whyte, W. F. 1984. *Learning from the Field: A Guide from Experience.* Beverly Hills.

Widner, J. A., ed. 1994. *Economic Change and Political Liberalization in Sub-Saharan Africa.* London.

Wilkin, P. 1996. "New Myths for the South: Globalization and the Conflict between Private Power and Freedom." *Third World Quarterly* 17, no. 2:228–38.

Williamson, J. G. 1996. "Globalization, Convergence, and History." *Journal of Economic History* 56, no. 2:277–306.

Wolff, J. H. 1992. "Zur langfristigen Wirtschaftsentwicklung der Dritten Welt." *Aus Politik und Zeitgeschichte* B50/92:24–30.

————. 1997. *Un demi-siècle de Nations Unies.* Série Seminaires et Colloques, no. 7. Marrakesh.

————. 2000. "Armutsbekämpfung durch Entwicklungshilfe: Probleme und Perspektiven." *Auspolitik und Zeitgeschichte* 9:26–31.

Wolin, S. 1960. *Politics and Vision.* Boston.